Golden Years of Fabergé

Drawings and Objects

from the Wigström Workshop

This book has been published with the support of
A La Vieille Russie, Est. 1851
Fabergé • Jewelry • Works of Art

Golden Years of Fabergé

Drawings and Objects
from the Wigström Workshop

Ulla Tillander-Godenhielm
Peter L. Schaffer
Alice Milica Ilich
Mark A. Schaffer

Foreword by A. Kenneth Snowman

Preface by Peter L. Schaffer

Editorial Director: Emmanuel Ducamp

A La Vieille Russie
&
Alain de Gourcuff Éditeur

Foreword

Since his passing in 1920, so much attention has been riveted, understandably enough, on the work of Carl Fabergé and his workshops, that for anything new of real historical value to be unearthed at this late stage must be regarded as genuinely exciting. As we all know only too well, good news these days is extremely thin on the ground, and especially where the question of aesthetics is involved.

Such was the discovery and eventual acquisition in 1986, almost by chance, of the two Holmström stock books, recording in richly illustrated detail all the business conducted by Albert Holmström's workshops from 6 March 1909 to 20 March 1915. Happily, they had been carefully preserved in the safe hands of charming descendants.

To have unearthed, a few years later, the actual working designs of the chief workmaster, Henrik Wigström, is quite simply miraculous. It has to be the most valuable discovery in this context since the death of the master, and the fact that it was the result of the research and probing curiosity of my dear friend Ulla Tillander-Godenhielm shows that, even today, justice can on rare occasions still prevail. As the saying goes, it couldn't have happened to a nicer girl! Messrs. Paul, Peter and Mark Schaffer have generously given their expertise to this book. Their family business A La Vieille Russie in New York has been dealing in Fabergé for three generations, and through the records of their firm they have managed to trace a good proportion of the beautiful objects illustrated in the Wigström archive. Without their kind help this book would not have been the same. The cooperation with Alice Ilich, with her unique expertise, has resulted in a quite invaluable work. After years of diligent and tireless study, it is splendid to see them — and all of, us rewarded in this way.

Under these uniquely special circumstances, I find it quite impossible to stop myself from repeating a favourite quotation, so singularly appropriate here. As Proust remarked so memorably, *"un petit croquis vaut mieux que le plus long discours"*; as you turn the pages that follow, the profound truth of this observation becomes abundantly clear.

I was first introduced to the extraordinary range of wonderfully conceived and expressed works by the St. Petersburg master as a child, when I recall my late father returning to London from his early pioneering trips to Russia, in the 1920's and right up to the outbreak of the Second World War, laden with treasures.

In the course of a long career as a tradesman in works of art, I have been privileged to have come across, and even to have acquired, quite a number of the actual objects produced from the designs that follow.

It was therefore especially thrilling to me to be in a position to examine the original water-coloured drawings which are so faithfully reproduced in the glamorous pages that follow.

A. KENNETH SNOWMAN

Preface

In the words of Fabergé himself: "Clearly, if you compare my things to those of such firms as Tiffany, Boucheron, and Cartier, you will find that the value of theirs is greater (than) that of mine. But of course these people were merchants and not "artist-jewelers". Expensive things interest me little if the value is merely in so many diamonds and pearls."

When the images in this book are viewed with Fabergé's statement in mind, its truth and validity shine through. And it is with these words in mind, as well as our long family association with Fabergé, that we are exceedingly pleased to work on the present album of Wigström, with its actual depictions of actual pieces in their actual sizes and their actual colors. The 'hand' of Wigström may be seen in his watercolors, and in the completed pieces made in his workshop. This is a rare discovery indeed, as the drawings in most of the other documents available are not at actual size, and show pieces obviously ordered in different materials. This album also demonstrates the great precision and care that helped to catapult Fabergé from the status of a small firm to that of a giant — of its time, and for all time. This care, precision and organization were adopted by Fabergé long before the term *quality circles* became synonymous with the transformation of the Japanese economy into a powerhouse of the last quarter of the twentieth century. In her essay on the Wigström workshop in this book, Ulla Tillander-Godenhielm discusses this ingenious method of production, and its repercussions on the quality, quantity and variety of Fabergé's *œuvre*. Fabergé had his own style, and even when some of his workmen also worked for others, the pieces they made for Fabergé invariably bear his "stylistic" signature. His work lay in the long tradition of great artist-jewelers such as Cellini, Dinglinger and Nitot. Most people in the field are aware to some extent of his working methods, but this book spells them out in unprecedented detail.

As many readers will know, A La Vieille Russie is a family firm founded in Kiev in 1851. In fact, the firm had two names, one French and one Russian. French was an important language in Russia and was the official Court language. English and German were also used but Russian, although used at Court, was often reserved for "naughty children". There, with two shops, it was placed among the top companies. Among the firm's clients was Fabergé, who made purchases of antiques that we like to think may have provided inspiration for some of his masterpieces.

When the firm moved to Paris, in 1921, ahead of the Soviet nationalization of private businesses, it became the focus of the Russian artistic and intellectual community in Paris.

Our firm's first shop in New York was opened as one of the first tenants in Rockefeller Center in 1933. It was a success, and in 1941 the name A La Vieille Russie was brought over, and the

Paris branch was closed ahead of the Nazi advance on the French capital. Being familiar already with the work of Fabergé, the firm started slowly to buy and sell examples of his *œuvre*. Our parents, Alexander and Ray Schaffer, were thus instrumental in the introduction of Fabergé to the United States. We had the three things necessary for a successful venture — quantity, quality and price! Fabergé was readily available, the price was right because the pieces were not that old and the quality was tops.

Today, still in New York, my brother and I operate the store together with Paul's son Mark. While our father was away on his many and lengthy buying trips (travel, especially to Russia, was difficult at best in those days), our mother helped to form the major collections that were to feature as the core of the *Fabergé in America* show that toured the United States to huge audiences. This was, in essence, a tribute to our parents and the collections they helped to form. Early clients included Matilda Geddings Gray, India Early Minshall, Lillian Thomas Pratt, and Marjorie Merriweather Post, all of whose collections today form part of major American museum collections. Without the assistance of our parents, these noted collections and many others would not have been formed. Over the years, we have been fortunate enough to handle twenty-three of the Imperial Eggs (about half of the number known to exist) along with scores of other pieces, including figurines, flowers, animals, frames and boxes of all types and sizes. In one of his "Fact and Comments" pieces in his magazine, the late Malcolm Forbes attributed to us over eighty percent of his collection. We are proud of our association both with these collections and with the many new ones being formed today.

This long history and reputation has assisted us in obtaining the privilege of including here new photographs of pieces from the Thai Royal Collection, as well as the loan of these same pieces for the exhibition that launched this publication. It was the first time that these pieces had been allowed to leave the Thai Royal Palace, and we are indeed honored to have been granted this privilege. The graciousness of Her Majesty Queen Sirikit in the production of this volume and exhibition was instrumental in its success. Her *Thai Support Foundation*, which benefits from this book, does a great deal for the Thai people and their native culture. In addition, we are proud to have received loans from the State Hermitage Museum, the Moscow Kremlin and Pavlovsk Palace among others, all of whom possess pieces depicted in the Wigström album. These pieces are included in this book.

Our parents would be greatly pleased that the "pebble" that they kicked at the top of the hill so long ago has become such a wonderful avalanche, resulting in important and scholarly research of a subject near and dear to them.

PETER L. SCHAFFER

Chapter One

Henrik Wigström
Portrait of a Master Craftsman

This book presents an album of drawings from the workshop of Henrik Wigström, Fabergé's leading workmaster from 1903 to 1918. The album came to light by pure chance a few years ago in a private home in Finland, where it had been neatly stored away in a bookcase and had laid untouched for decades. The owners, who were friends and former neighbors of the Wigström family, had long forgotten its very existence. But happily people occasionally spring-clean their bookshelves. And happily too, they are curious about their possessions. Thus the album was brought to me for inspection.

The Wigström album

I shall long remember the thrill on first opening this hefty volume. My eyes met a galaxy of watercolors showing the most mesmerizing objects, including perfume bottles, *étuis*, frames, lorgnettes, parasol handles, cigarette cases, letter openers, and Easter eggs. It did not take long to realize that I held a rare workshop document from the House of Fabergé in my hands — and not only was it rare but also important, in view of the scanty nature of information on the workshops that had been available hitherto.

The Wigström album now makes a wonderful complement to the richly illustrated stock books for the years 1909 to 1915 from the neighboring workshop of Albert Holmström, discovered some ten years ago.[1]

At the time of writing, the Holmström stock books and the Wigström album remain the only surviving documentary material produced

The Wigström album was used in the atelier as a reference book against which working designs could be checked. This drawing of a table clock in nephrite and gold is taken from plate 305.

A few years ago, a rare album of drawings and some working designs from the workshop of Henrik Wigström, Fabergé's chief workmaster, came to light in a private home in Finland.

A gum pot in translucent white enamel on a *guilloché* ground, the gadrooned gold brush with an amethyst finial.

PLATE 5

Drawings of scent bottles and gum pots in hardstone or crystal with enameled lids.

The plate numbers used in the Wigström album have been retained here, and the plates are shown in their original sequence. Plates not reproduced at full-page size are included in the appendices. Plate references in the text and captions always apply to the album.

by the workshops themselves. The memoirs of Fabergé's head designer, Franz Birbaum, contain a fund of inside information concerning the firm as a whole.[2] To this is now added illuminating data regarding the goldsmiths' trade, now discovered on an almost daily basis in Russia's newly opened archives.

The discovery of the Wigström album has inspired the authors of this book in many ways. First and foremost, it has inspired us to look into the ingenious methods of production developed by Fabergé in collaboration with his skilled craftsmen. In a relatively brief period, the company grew from a rather insignificant traditional jeweler into an industrial enterprise with some 500 employees, most of whom were engaged in the production process. The workmanship was always of a superlative quality, and each completed piece was unique. One of the firm's marketing slogans, indeed, claimed that two identical pieces would never be produced. This rapidly growing business clearly required new and rationalized production methods. Mechanization, specialization, serial production of various parts and details, and above all a cleverly orchestrated team-based approach among the craftsmen: these were the secrets that lay behind Fabergé's production during the first decade of the twentieth century. So successful were Fabergé and his extraordinary team that each object made in these avant-garde *ateliers* retains the feeling of being the work of a single pair of hands, from start to finish. It is this quality that continuously arouses the astonishment of Fabergé — including even those who are themselves trained goldsmiths.

The Wigström album illustrates some one thousand pieces produced for Fabergé by the workshop between 1911 and 1916, the majority falling within the years 1911 to 1913. The pieces are drawn at their actual size, in

A gum pot (Pl. 5) carved in bowenite in the shape of a pear. The enameled stem serves the double purpose of lid and brush.

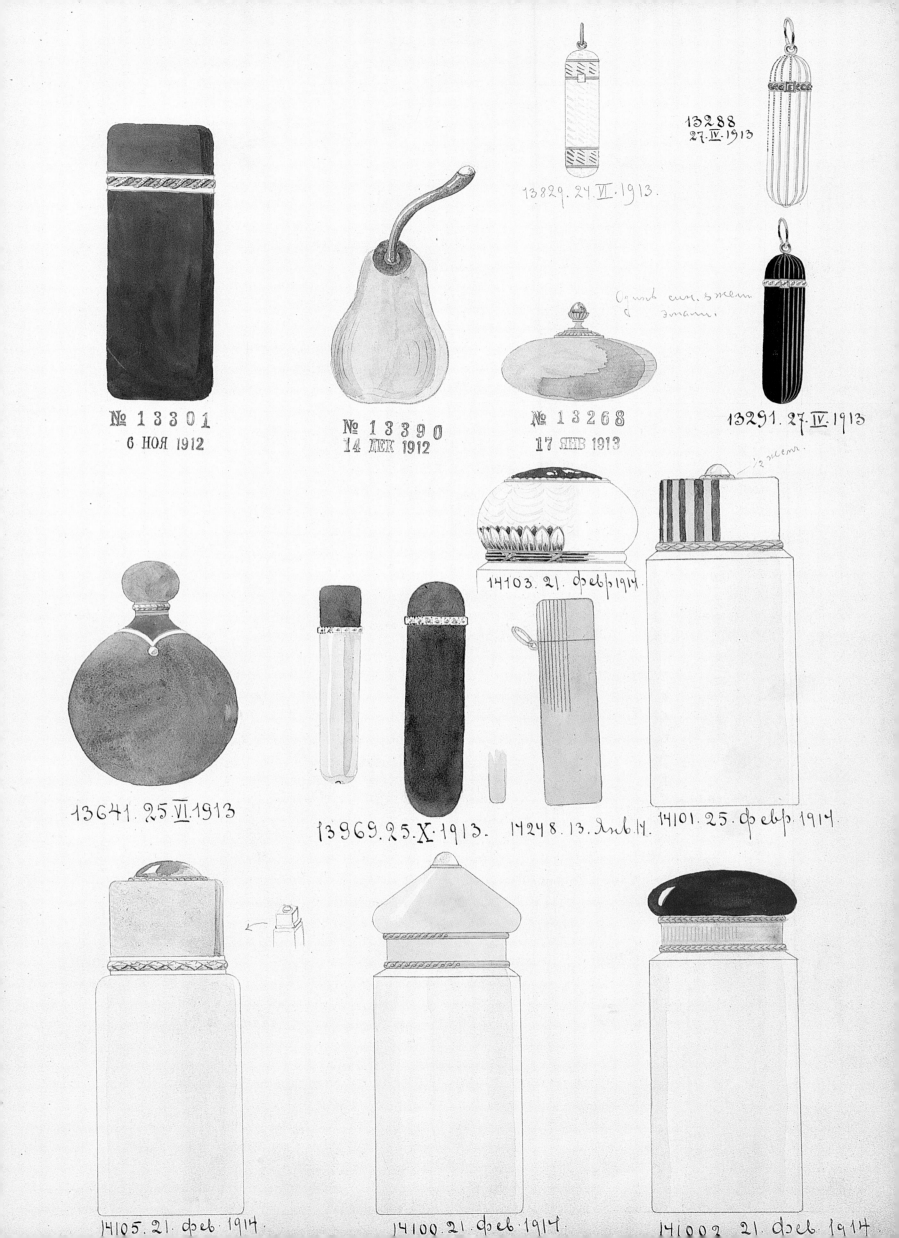

№ 13301
6 НОЯ 1912

№ 13390
14 ДЕК 1912

№ 13268
17 ЯНВ 1913

13288
27·IV·1913

13829. 24·VI·1913.

Одинъ сик. въ жел. этаж.

13291. 27·IV·1913

13641. 25·VI·1913

13969. 25·X·1913.

14103. 21. февр 1914

½ жел.

14248. 13. Янв. 14.

14101. 25. февр. 1914.

14105. 21. февр 1914.

14100. 21. февр. 1914.

14102. 21. февр. 1914.

Drawing of a nephrite frame in the neo-classical style. It bears the monogram H W, indicating that it was designed by Henrik Wigström himself, and contains his portrait, so that the goldsmith could feel the gaze of his workmaster on his shoulders...

pencil, pen and ink, and in nearly all cases colored in watercolors. Anyone familiar with Fabergé's work cannot fail to be delighted by the accuracy and detail of these drawings. The technique and material of every piece is clearly evident, whether it be engine turning (*guilloché*), enameling, a cabochon ruby set in the thumbpiece of a cigarette case, or the use of a Siberian hardstone or multicolored gold. Most of the sketches include a date of completion, indicating that the drawing has a finished object as its counterpart. This knowledge immediately sparked off a fascinating treasure hunt of existing objects. Quite a number have already been located, in museums and private homes, virtually throughout the world.

The main function of the Wigström album was to serve as a reference catalog for the *atelier*. The finely rendered and detailed illustrations showing the wide range of models previously produced by the workshop served as useful guidelines for future production. For the purposes of the craftsmen at the bench, however, there were separate designs and working drawings. Beneath each drawing in the album is a production number. This production number, used internally by the workshop, should not be confused with the inventory number, which was scratched on each object as it was entered into the sales ledgers.

It has also been the ambition of the authors to include in this work the personal story of the master craftsman Henrik Wigström, a protagonist of great importance "behind the scenes", who richly deserves to be lifted into the limelight. Fabergé literature has tended to focus, and rightly so, on the mastermind of the renowned Court Jeweler Carl Fabergé himself. The matter of how the

Overleaf:

PLATE 25

Drawings of
fan mounts enriched
with classical motifs.

PLATE 41

Drawings of jeweled
and enameled
lorgnettes. The lorgnette
at bottom left is in the
Louis XV style, a rather
unusual feature
in Wigström's work
and much more
closely associated
with that of his mentor,
Mikhail Perkhin.

objects were produced, and by whom, has been somewhat overlooked in the extraordinary saga of the House of Fabergé. But this is not to say that the craftsmen and their work are not appreciated: in the words of Henry C. Bainbridge, Fabergé's first biographer: "Without the workmasters and workmen, he [Carl Fabergé] could have done nothing. What he conceived they carried into effect."[3]

Henrik Wigström was one of the leading players in this remarkable process. He was in charge of the *atelier* that was entrusted with the firm's most prestigious commissions. His importance to the House was recognized by Bainbridge: "Indeed today his name, among collectors and art dealers, is as much a household one as that of Fabergé himself."[4]

The young apprentice

Henrik Immanuel Wigström (1862-1923), was the son of a Finnish churchwarden. The family lived in Tammisaari, an idyllic town on the southern coast of Finland. Though small and remote, the town was fortunate enough to be home to Petter Madsén, a successful manufacturer of silverware who was familiar with the jewelry trade in St. Petersburg, as at one time he had had a workshop there. In his homeland, Madsén worked as a subcontractor for Russian retail jewelers, and thus retained his excellent contacts in the Russian capital. Henrik Wigström was apprenticed to Madsén at the age of ten. The boy's father had just died, leaving a destitute widow with four small children to support. Once in Madsén's employment, his master's trade with Russia, as well as his numerous business contacts there, awakened in the young Henrik a desire to work in St. Petersburg. On becoming a journeyman at the age of sixteen, he accordingly applied for the official documents needed for a prolonged stay in Russia.[5] Armed with his passport,

Two drawings and
a corresponding scent flask
(Pl. 7). The body of the
flask is of translucent white
enamel with moss
agate plaques within
a rose-cut diamond border.

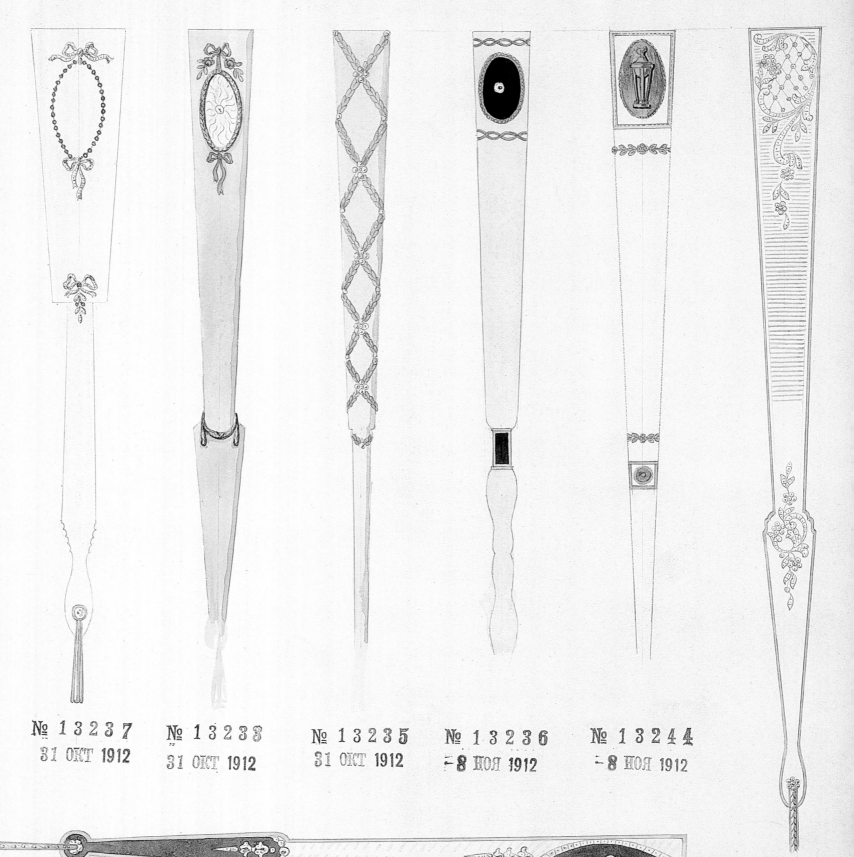

№ 13237
31 ОКТ 1912

№ 13233
31 ОКТ 1912

№ 13235
31 ОКТ 1912

№ 13236
- 8 НОЯ 1912

№ 13244
- 8 НОЯ 1912

13690 22. XI. 1913

13688. 27. VI. 1

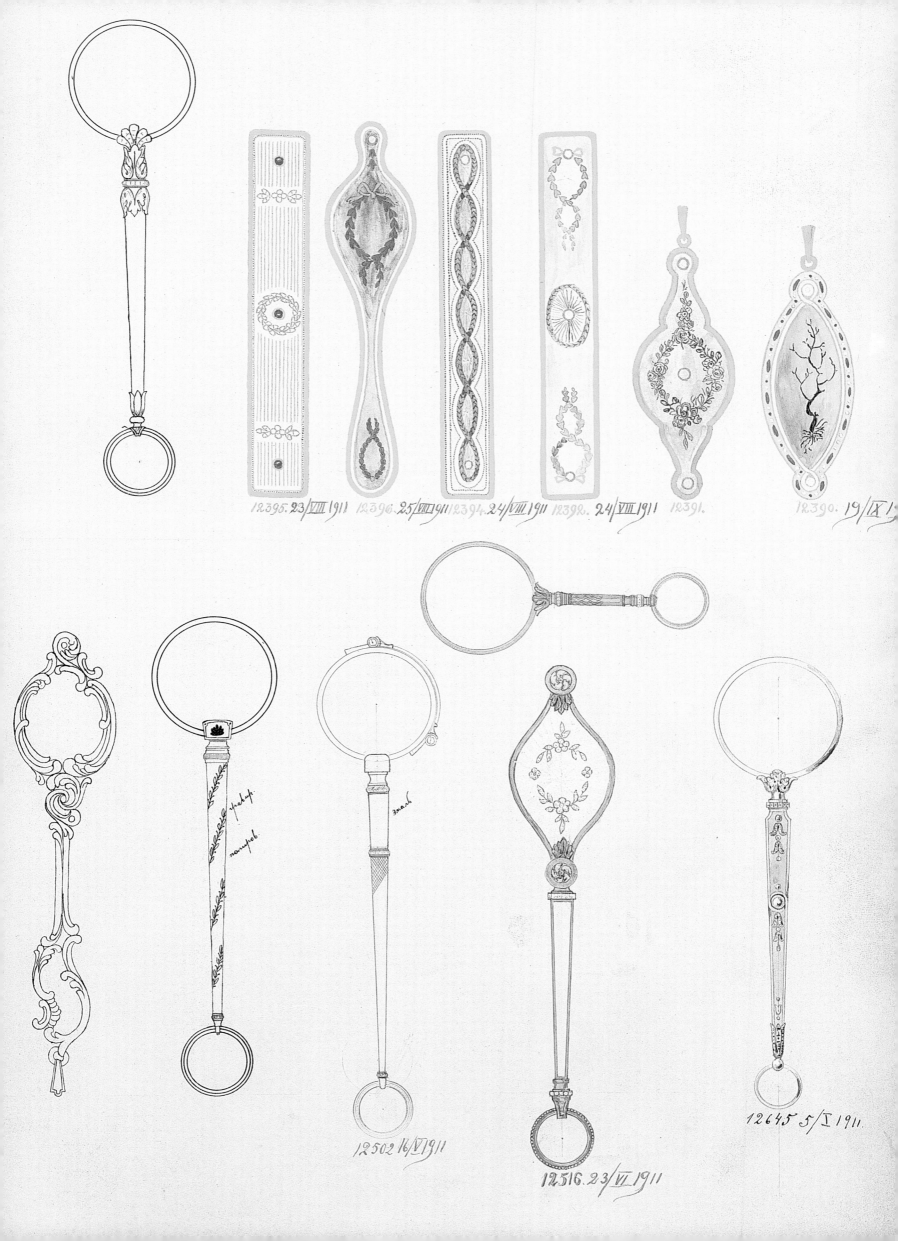

12395. 23/VIII 1911   12396. 25/VII 1911   12394. 24/VIII 1911   12392. 24/VIII 1911   12391.   12390. 19/IX 1

12502 16/V 1911

12516. 23/VI 1911

12645 5/X 1911

he embarked on a cart laden with farm produce for the markets of St. Petersburg.[6] We do not know who employed Wigström on his arrival in the capital, but we do know that by the year 1884, at the age of twenty-two, he was on the payroll of the master goldsmith Mikhail Evlampievich Perkhin (1860-1903), whose shop at this time was already working exclusively for Fabergé. Wigström was fortunate, for Carl Fabergé and his brother Agathon[7] recognized the extraordinary potential talent of the young master and his journeyman, and devoted much time to encouraging their skills and developing the collaboration between the workshop and themselves. Only two years younger than Perkhin, Wigström soon became his right-hand man, and the two of them formed an excellent team. By the late 1880s, Perkhin's workshop was Fabergé's most exacting production unit.

A new concept

Over the two decades from 1880 to 1900, the House of Fabergé grew from a modest goldsmiths into an important emporium, and from craftsmen of traditional jewelry to a large-scale manufacturer of a wide range of products of the goldsmith's art. In 1885, Carl Fabergé was granted the title "Supplier to the Imperial Court".

Expanding their output called for more efficient manufacturing processes and modernization, and the important decision was taken to out-source production. The workmasters of the various *ateliers* were helped to become independent entrepreneurs. The idea of offering masters ownership of their workshops within a system of close cooperation was an ingenious one. It provided many advantages, both for the House of Fabergé and for the individual workmasters, securing long-term cooperation between the parties involved. For the master, it provided a guarantee of a steady outlet for his

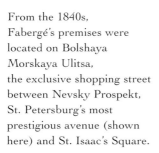

From the 1840s, Fabergé's premises were located on Bolshaya Morskaya Ulitsa, the exclusive shopping street between Nevsky Prospekt, St. Petersburg's most prestigious avenue (shown here) and St. Isaac's Square.

Carl Fabergé sorting gemstones. His genius lay in his ability both to respond to his clients' tastes and to work in close collaboration with masters such as Henrik Wigström.

production, quite apart from the motivation of being his own boss. Long before the modern concept of industrial democracy was conceived, its prototype was thus at work at Fabergé. Paradoxically, it came to the fore during the reign of the greatest autocracy the world has ever known.

The recruitment and training of workmen was an important responsibility of the workmasters. The masters were also responsible for the quality of their workmanship and for guaranteeing that the terms and times of delivery were respected. In return, they were granted the right to mark their products with their own initials.

The system of out-sourcing freed Fabergé's management from the burden of trivial day-to-day problems. The benefits of workmaster-owned shops are especially evident from a reading of the annual business reports of the goldsmith Alexander Tillander.[8] These include repeated laments as to the difficulties of recruiting suitable apprentices and journeymen and the problem of keeping the skilled ones on the staff. Some of Tillander's craftsmen suffered from a chronic drinking problem, moreover, which kept them away from their benches, often at times when the workshop was already understaffed, such as before Christmas or Easter. The constant turnover of staff, frequently including workmasters and designers, meant that much of the owners' potentially creative time was wasted on dealing with unproductive matters.

By the late 1890s, Fabergé had become the most important jeweler in St. Petersburg, employing some five hundred artists, craftsmen and sales staff.[9] As the company operated from several addresses, much time and energy was wasted in traffic between the various sites. It soon became

To house his shop, workshops and workmasters' living quarters all under one roof — a very innovative concept — Carl Fabergé had a new building erected on Bolshaya Morskaya Street in 1900 in an eclectic style.

Henrik Wigström's workshop, located on the second floor of the Fabergé building, contained eight workbenches, each seating seven or eight craftsmen.

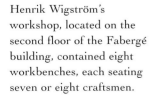

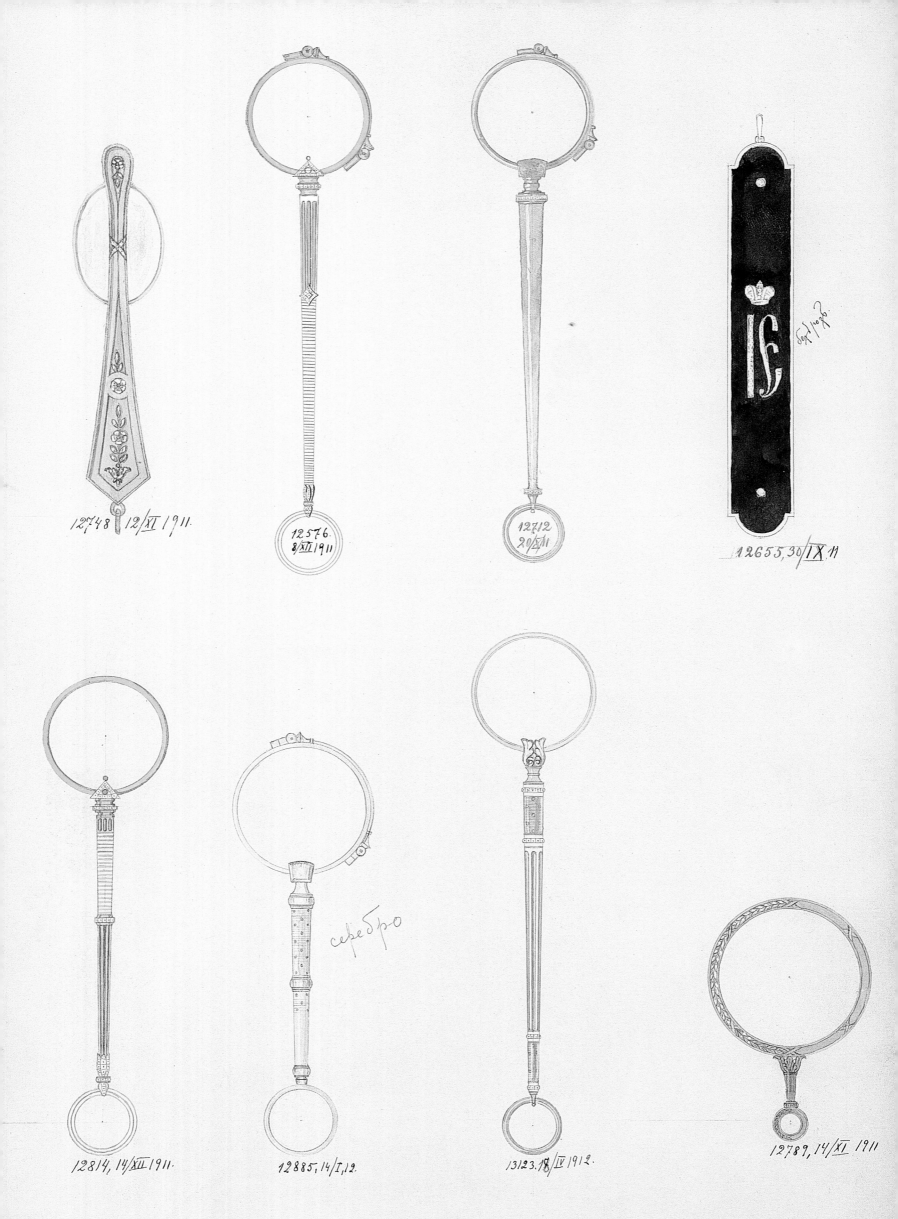

12748, 12/XII 1911.

12576. 8/XII 1911

12712 20/II 11

без проб.

12655, 30/IX 11

12814, 14/XII 1911.

серебро

12885, 14/I.12.

13123, 18/IV 1912.

12789, 14/XII 1911

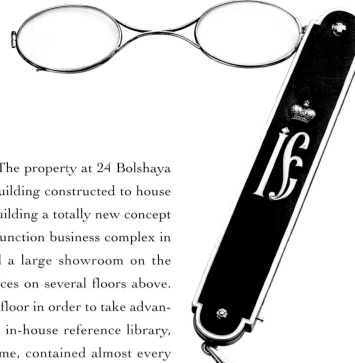

necessary to make production more efficient. The property at 24 Bolshaya Morskaya Street was purchased, and a new building constructed to house most of the company's operations. With this building a totally new concept was born, for this was the very first multiple-function business complex in Russia. On completion in 1900, it provided a large showroom on the ground floor, facing the main street, with offices on several floors above. The designers' studios were housed on the top floor in order to take advantage of as much natural light as possible. An in-house reference library, unique in a business establishment at that time, contained almost every known book on the goldsmith's and lapidary's craft.

The right-hand wing of the building that stood in the courtyard was given over to the production units. Direct access from this wing to the offices and studios of the main building facilitated the frequent communications between the firm's various departments. In the tradition of the old guild system,[10] under which the master lived in close proximity to the workshop, Carl Fabergé moved his home into the building.[11] An apartment for the chief workmaster was also included, annexed to the workshop itself.

Grand Duchess Elizaveta Feodorovna's lorgnette, with the Monogram IE on one side, standing for *Igumena* (Abbess) Elizaveta. Following her husband's assassination in 1905, the Grand Duchess had taken the veil and founded a convent in Moscow.

The workshops

The five floors of the courtyard wing housed the main workshops. From 1903 onwards, the chief workshop of which Wigström was in charge was on the second floor. Beneath this lay Hollming's *atelier*, on the first floor, and Armfelt's on the ground floor. Above the chief workshop was Holmström's *atelier*, with Thielemann's workshop on the top floor. Elsewhere in the building was a case-maker's workshop.[12]

The spacious workshops were furnished with traditional kidney-shaped workbenches, placed in a row next to the large windows. There was room

Gold lorgnette with a deep gray translucent enamel collar over a *guilloché* ground. A pushpiece below the lens snaps the lens open.

Grand Duchess Elizaveta Feodorovna (Ella), sister of Empress Alexandra Feodorovna. She was married to the Emperor's uncle Grand Duke Sergei Alexandrovich, Governor-General of Moscow.

A lorgnette in platinum created in the Wigström workshop in October 1912.

for some eight workbenches, each seating seven or eight craftsmen, so that each workshop could employ up to 64 people. The craftsmen engaged in manual work were seated at the workbenches in groups, according to the particular nature of their work.

In Wigström's shop, the men engaged in all-round goldsmith's work sat together, with next to them the mounters of hardstone objects, gem-setters, embossers, and engravers.

Set along the wall opposite the workbenches were the machinery and equipment necessary for the daily work routine. The Wigström workshop was equipped with its own oven for melting small quantities of gold, a large draw plate for drawing and twisting wire, a steel-rolling mill for thinning and stretching metal, and anvils for the working of sheet metal. One of the most important tools was the *guilloché* machine, which required a highly proficient operating crew as the turning process was very demanding. There were also a number of polishing machines, manned by specially appointed polishers, while on the wall opposite the embossers and engravers was a shelf holding a collection of wax models of ancient classical ornaments, used extensively by the ornamenters in their work.[13]

At the front end of the workshop was the large office occupied by the workmaster, his assistant and his clerks, which was also furnished with two desks and a large table for the workshop designer. This was where the sorting, measuring, and weighing of gemstones took place, and where work was allotted to the various craftsmen. On one wall was a set of shelves holding the production ledgers: this is where the album presented in this book would have been kept.

The craftsmen of the workshop were a highly heterogeneous group, brought together from all corners of the Russian Empire and representing

The drawing taken from plate 45, showing the platinum lorgnette illustrated on this page.

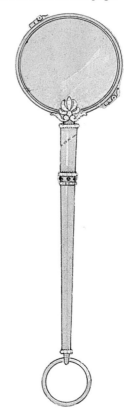

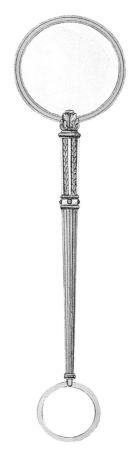

its wide spectrum of different cultures, religions, and tongues. They also differed widely in age, from the very young to the very old. But in spite of all these differences, testimony from goldsmiths who worked there, both oral and written, indicates that there were few problems among the staff at Fabergé.

This good working morale and high degree of motivation was largely due to the enlightened system by which the head of each workshop took a personal interest in each member of his staff, guiding them and discussing the work in hand. This philosophy of "staff welfare" pervaded the entire firm, creating a feeling that all the workers were members of an extended family. First-hand testimony of the encouraging atmosphere at Fabergé comes from the memoirs of the engraver Jalmari Haikonen, who worked for Wigström: "There was a custom in the House of Fabergé, that when something especially fine had been completed, the Director and the workmaster in charge took the object around the shops. They showed it at each workbench, saying: 'Here is the masterpiece, ready now!' By this means I came to see some of the finest pieces made in the House. One day in early 1916, I cannot remember the exact day, they showed us a glorious masterpiece which had been completed in our workshop. It was a commission from the

A drawing of a lorgnette in gold with bands of laurel leaves (Pl. 45).

Fragments and semi-manufactured objects from the personal workbench of Henrik Wigström, showing various stages in the completion process. They include a mold for a rabbit's head shown on plate 191.

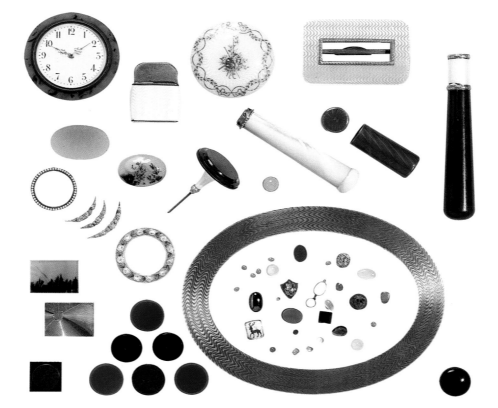

The son of a Finnish churchwarden, Henrik Wigström had arrived in St. Petersburg in the 1870s, rapidly to find himself the assistant of Carl Fabergé's main collaborator Mikhail Perkhin, before succeeding him in 1903.

Emperor himself, a snuffbox in platinum. I had seen it being made — it weighed about half a kilogram. On the lid was the large monogram "N II", set with enormous diamonds. In each corner were double-headed eagles, also set with large diamonds. This was to be a gift to the Emperor's uncle, Commander-in-Chief of the Armies, Grand Duke Nikolai Nikolaievich. We saw it when it was completed, lying in its fitted case, a superb piece, all in platinum."[14]

The guild system was abolished in Russia at the end of the nineteenth century, but the traditions and working practices that it had established were by that time so deeply rooted in the routines of workshops dependent largely on manual labor that they continued to be observed by the masters. An important legacy from the old system was the tradition of training apprentices. These young craftsmen-to-be were appointed to the workshops at a very young age: an apprentice of a mere ten or eleven years old was not an unusual sight at a St. Petersburg workbench at that time.[15] The boy was seated at the bench next to his instructor, a master goldsmith or journeyman. This would be his seat for the next six years, the average length of an apprenticeship in a goldsmith's workshop. The teaching method was simple. From the outset, apprentices were expected to learn by watching their instructors at work, and by their own innumerable mistakes. It was a method that required a great deal of patience on both sides, as the instructors were inevitably concerned principally with the work in hand, with the teaching of their apprentices taking second place.

Naturally, the presence of young children in the workplace was not without its problems. Traditionally, the proximity of the master's home was a great advantage, as his wife could be called in to help out. In the heyday of

Henrik Wigström's wife, Ida, was in charge of the housekeeping and the day-to-day upbringing of their four children.

the guild system, apprentices and young unmarried journeymen had lived as part of the master's household, and his wife had always taken an active part in the workshop. From 1900 to 1918 Henrik Wigström and his family followed this tradition, making their home in the Fabergé building, on the same floor as the workshop. From her windows, Mrs. Wigström had a clear view down the whole length of the workshop, the distance across the yard being a little over twenty yards. Mrs. Ida Wigström, Finnish-born like her husband Henrik, had come to St. Petersburg as a very young girl in search of work, and met her future husband at the Finnish Church, a meeting place for young migrants. Their complementary personalities made them an ideal couple. He had a big heart and was sometimes far too generous for her taste, and he liked having fun and making practical jokes. She was fiercly practical, took life seriously, and took charge of the housekeeping and the day-to-day upbringing of their four growing children. Ida's principle that "the boys should be spanked twice a day, but the girls only once", has passed into family folklore.[16] Henrik's successful career, and the prosperity it brought, was gradually reflected in the family's lifestyle and in their two homes. Detailed records of the furnishings of the Wigström apartment reveal a home typical of the St. Petersburg *petite bourgeoisie* of the time, with a drawing room, a dining room, a sanctum for the man of the house, four bedrooms and a kitchen. Pride of place in the drawing room went to a grand piano and a large and costly *chiffonnier*.[17] In addition, the Wigström family built themselves a house in the country: a comfortable two-story wooden building, some forty-five minutes by train from St. Petersburg, over the border in the Grand Duchy of Finland. Their close neighbors there were the celebrated

Lyyli, Hellin, Henrik Wilhelm and Yrjö Wigström (from right to left) were brought up in the Bolshaya Morskaya building from 1900. Associated with the workshop's practices at an early age, Lyyli and Henrik Wilhelm became their father's assistants.

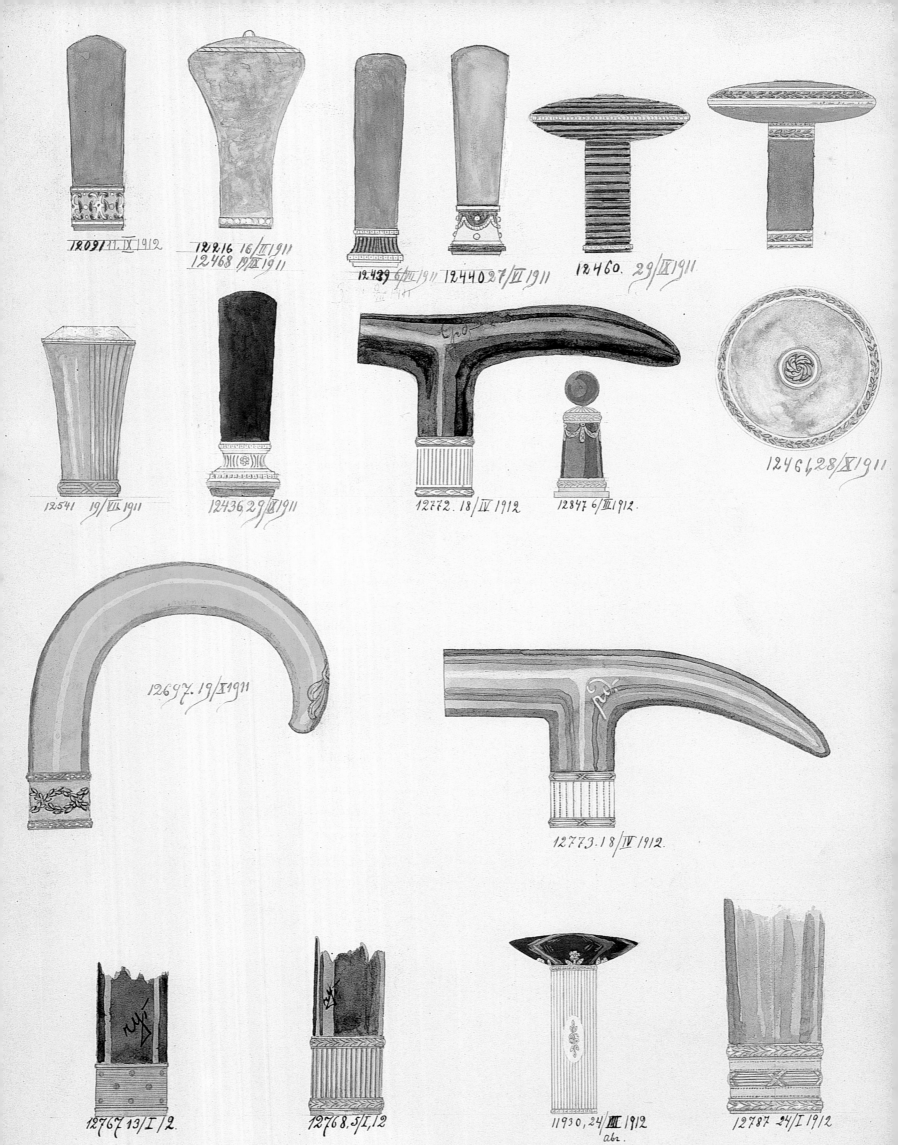

12091 11. IX 1912

12216 16/II 1911
12468 19/IX 1911

12439 6/II 1911   12440 27/VI 1911   12460. 29/IX 1911

12541   19/VII 1911   12436 29/IX 1911   12772. 18/IV 1912   12847 6/III 1912.   12461 28/IX 1911

12697. 19/X 1911

12773. 18/IV 1912.

12767 13/I /2.   12768, 5/I,12   11930, 24/III 1912 ab.   12787 24/I 1912

PLATE 61

Drawings of hardstone
and enameled cane handles,
most of them with details
in the neo-classical style.

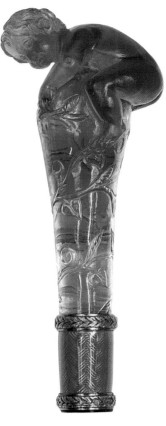

Russian painter Ilya Repin and Carl Fabergé's son, Agathon Karlovich. Here, close to the sandy beaches of the resort of Terijoki, the Wigströms spent Christmas, Easter and the summer holidays.

Fin-de-siècle Russia offered no retirement system, so goldsmiths' workshops included many craftsmen of advanced age: "One [polisher] was a grey-headed man, he said he had come to the house at the age of 25. Now he was 82. He said he was pleased with his life. Of that I am sure. Behind me sat a man on his own. He was 72. He spent a long time working with his chasing hammer on a silver tea-glass holder. He had worked on it for two months at least." [18] Here is evidence of the benevolence of the firm's system, which allowed the old craftsmen to remain at work, even though they were no longer able to work efficiently.

Surprisingly, the least significant problem among this polyglot group of many different nationalities proved to be that of the language they spoke amongst themselves. Over two centuries, a common vocabulary had evolved in the workshops of St. Petersburg: the Esperanto of the goldsmith's world, it consisted of words borrowed from German, Russian and French. A few examples of this cosmopolitan argot have been preserved to this day, and make highly entertaining reading. [19]

A parasol handle carved
in smoky quartz with
a cherub surmounting floral
motifs, over a gold-bordered
pink *guilloché* enamel
collar (see similar handles
on plate 67, page 35).

Daily life at the Wigström workshop

The Wigström workshop was a "family affair", an arrangement that was by no means unusual among Fabergé's workshops: the *ateliers* of Holmström, Hollming, Wäkevä and Thielemann, all already had two generations of the same family working together. Sons were apprenticed at the shop with a view to taking over from their fathers; clever daughters, if they were so inclined, were employed as designers or clerks.

A compact in dark pink
enamel, a variant of the blue
example drawn on plate 61
(opposite).

Drawing of a blue *guilloché* enamel parasol handle with the crowned initial T, most probably a gift to Princess Tatiana Konstantinovna, daughter of Grand Duke Konstantin Konstantinovich.

Henrik Wigström had himself been the close assistant of his predecessor, Mikhail Perkhin, for seventeen years. Not only did the two masters work well together, but a warm friendship also developed between their two families. Perkhin and his wife, Tatiana Vladimirovna, were even godparents to the Wigström children. But when Perkhin died prematurely at the age of forty-three, his workshop unaccountably passed to Wigström, without any payment in return.

This greatly surprised his colleagues, particularly in view of the fact that Perkhin's adolescent son thereby lost his inheritance.[20] The takeover apparently came about on the personal initiative of Carl Fabergé, and was prompted by his concern to ensure that this essential workshop should not suffer a transition period at a time when the business was growing so dynamically. On a professional level Henrik Wigström had proved himself worthy of carrying on Perkhin's fine work, and his disinherited son was undoubtedly compensated in some other way.

The Wigström children more or less grew up in the workshop milieu. Family life centered around activities associated with their father's work, as was the case for the families of most of the goldsmiths and other craftsmen emerging from the old guild system.

Lyyli, Wigström's eldest daughter, always treasured childhood memories of her father's work, especially of the more important commissions. She remembered, for example, being taken by her father to the Imperial stables at the age of twelve, in 1897, in order to study in detail the upholstery of the coronation coach seats and check the shade of red used in the fabric. This was the coach that had carried Empress Alexandra Feodorovna to the coronation at the Cathedral of Resurrection in Moscow the previous year. The Easter egg to be given by Nicholas II to Alexandra that year was the

Drawing of a cane handle possibly in Karelian birch, with an opaque white enamel collar (Pl. 63).

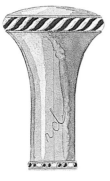

Drawing of a cane handle in hardstone (aventurine or rhodonite), very popular among Russian clients (Pl. 63)

Drawing of a hardstone cane handle, showing the internal workshop price code (Pl. 63).

Drawing of a cane handle in red gold with an elegantly fluted décor (Pl. 63).

Fabergé Coronation Egg, and the surprise within it was to be a model in miniature of the coronation coach. Shortly before Easter the miniature coach was at its enameling stage, and the enamelers needed to know the exact shade of "raspberry red" required.[21]

Lyyli Wigström found it natural to start her working career as an employee of the workshop, entering the business soon after leaving school, at the age of seventeen. This was in 1902, a year before Perkhin's death. Her first tasks in the workshop were simple ones, but eventually she was entrusted with the gemstone stock, with responsibility for allocating the stones and keeping detailed records. Her other duties included keeping the books, among them, the albums of drawings.

Lyyli's younger brother Henrik Wilhelm Wigström also came to work in the shop, starting his apprenticeship in 1905 at the age of sixteen, and under the supervision of his father becoming a journeyman and then a master goldsmith. Having trained in the workshop for ten years, he was promoted to become his father's assistant. This was in 1915, three years before the Bolsheviks closed down the firm of Fabergé and its workshops.

The working day in *fin-de-siècle* St. Petersburg was a long one, starting at seven in the morning and finishing around six in the evening, with an hour-long break for lunch. On Saturdays, work finished around three in the afternoon. Before Christmas and Easter, the craftsmen were at their benches from very early in the morning to late at night, including Saturdays and Sundays. When the workshop was under-staffed during these rush periods, the journeymen were encouraged to take their work home with them.[22]

The early morning routine at Wigström's was always the same. The starting signal for the day was the clang of the iron doors of the safe being

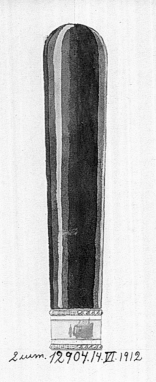

2шт. 12904. 14.VI.1912.

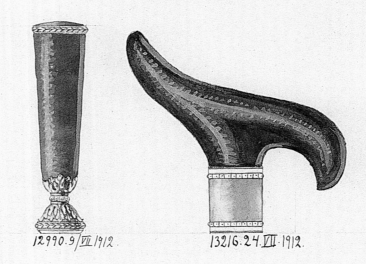

12990. 9/VII 1912.

13216. 24.VII. 1912.

№ 13320   № 1332

18 ОКТ 1912

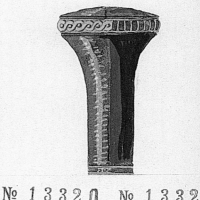

№ 13272

18 ОКТ 1912

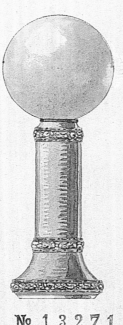

№ 13271

25 ОКТ 1912

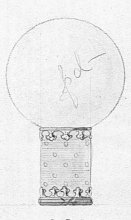

№ 12820

31 ОКТ 1912

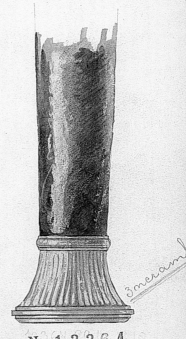

№ 13364

29 НОЯ 1912

13343. 13.II.1913.

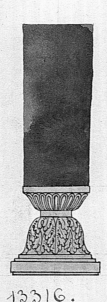

13316.

13685. 27.VI.1913.

4.X.1913.

PLATE 65

Drawings of cane handles and hand seals in hardstone or *guilloché* enamel.

A hand seal in blue and white enamel on a *guilloché* ground (Pl. 65).

opened, as the craftsmen lined up to receive their "iron boxes", kept overnight in the safe. Each journeyman had his own box containing his personal tools and the piece he was working on, together with a profusion of precious metal parts and wire, all of which were necessary for the smooth progress of the work.

The workmaster was constantly busy organizing the production of his *atelier*. Much of his time and energy was devoted to the famous "round table" discussions instituted under Carl Fabergé, at which all the key figures in the production process came together and the manufacturing strategies of the House were hammered out.

The production line

Each workshop of the House of Fabergé had its own specialty, with production divided between them accordingly. The Wigström workshop, being the principal one, was allocated the most exacting commissions, especially important pieces for the Imperial family.

Before he became chief workmaster, Henrik Wigström assisted Perkhin in making twenty-six Imperial Easter eggs and after his promotion, he supervised a further twenty.

But the mainstay of the firm's production were functional pieces and *objets de fantaisie*. The Wigström album includes up to fifty different types of product made in the workshop. As models were hardly ever repeated, this highlights the truly impressive organizational genius of Fabergé's production methods.

A wide range of boxes of all possible kinds — table boxes, snuffboxes, pill boxes and *bonbonnières* — was one of Wigström's specialties, while cigarette

A triple nephrite seal mounted in varicolored gold. It was designed to appear as a single seal but reveals within the mount three seal stones, in bloodstone, carnelian, and agate (Pl. 65).

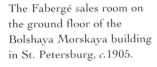

The Fabergé sales room on the ground floor of the Bolshaya Morskaya building in St. Petersburg, *c.*1905.

PLATE 67

Drawings of hand seals, and parasol and cane handles, featuring the parasol handle illustrated below.

A topaz handle carved in the shape of a fabulous fish in the Chinese taste, with a pink *guilloché* enamel collar. It is now in the collection of the State Hermitage Museum in St. Petersburg. Another example is shown on plate 67.

cases constituted the largest single category of work. A steady stream of these *portcigar*, the Russian word for boxes for both cigars and cigarettes, passed through the workshop: "...ten men were concentrated on producing nothing but cigarette cases. Different models and shapes, most of them in 56 *zolotniks*, the equivalent of 14-carat gold, some in 72, the equivalent of 18-carat, some in multicolored gold. Some were engraved by hand, others engine-turned. At times there was a good 40 cases waiting in our engravers' line. One man did the *guilloché* work, we engravers repaired and corrected the traces of the machine. The polishers gave the cases a final rub."[23]

One constant and vital duty of the chief master was the development of new manufacturing processes. Semi-manufactured products proved one important way of cutting material and labor costs, and were introduced to an increasing extent into the predominantly manual working processes. Fittings and findings of all kinds were prefabricated by subcontractors, including all attachments for pinning or fastening, such as hinges, loops, catches, snaps, and clasps. Chain work and gold mesh for jeweled evening bags, very much in vogue at the time, were produced by the workshop of Feodor Andreievich Rutsch.[24] Strips and bands of delicate laurel or acanthus leaves, palmettes in multicolored gold, garlands, ribbons, rosettes, and miniature roses used in ornamentation were all pressed in moulds. Small figurines in the round were cast in gold or silver using the lost-wax or *cire perdue* process. Such methods of speeding up and facilitating production were by no means an invention of the Fabergé workshops, for they had been used by goldsmiths for centuries — but now in St. Petersburg they were honed to perfection.

A collection of semi-manufactured objects and fragments of precious material, from the personal workbench of the master craftsman, has by pure

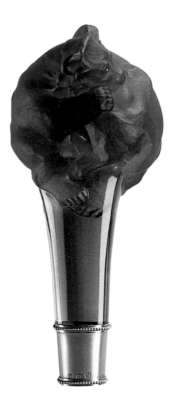

A parasol handle carved in smoky quartz in the shape of two cuddling bear cubs. Originally in the study of Nicholas II in the Alexander Palace at Tsarsköe Selo, it is now in the Armory Museum at the Moscow Kremlin (Pl. 67).

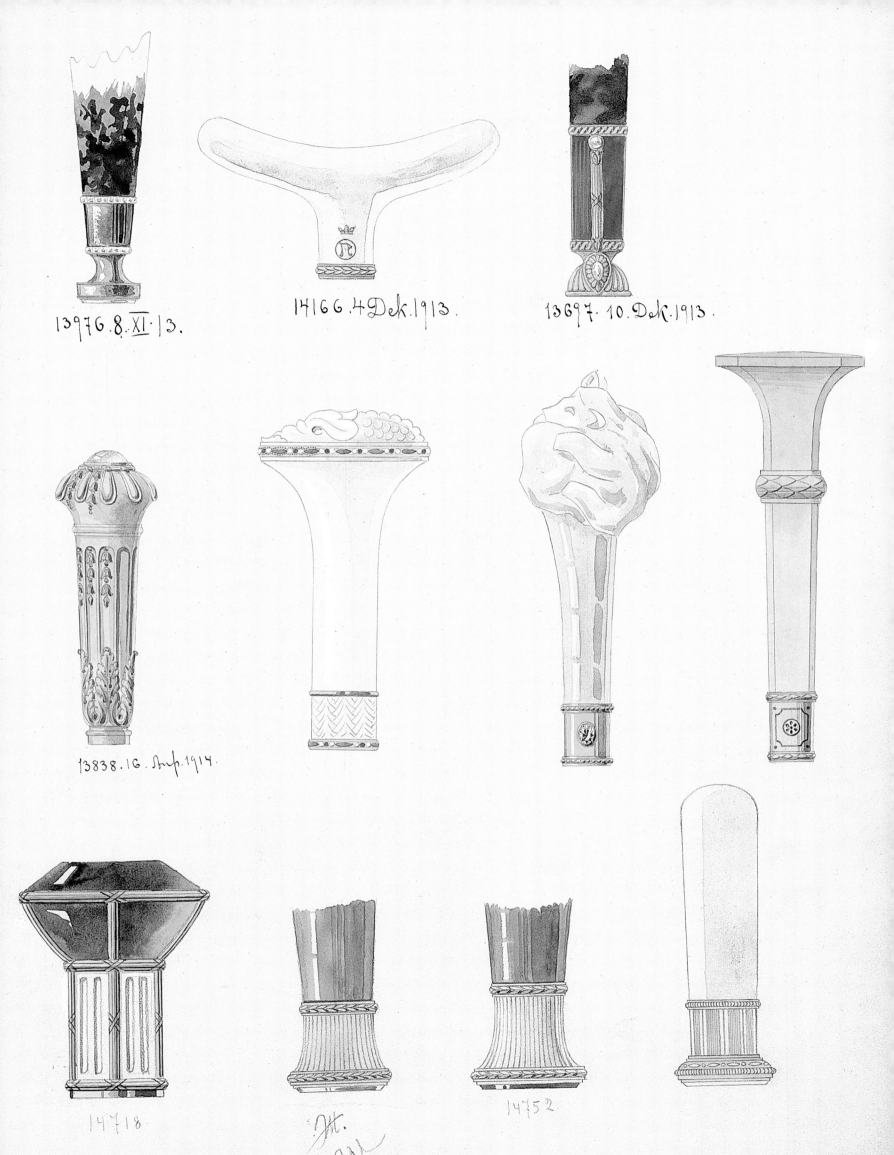

13976. 8. XI. 13.

14166. 4 Dek. 1913.

13697. 10. Dek. 1913.

13838. 16. Anp. 1914.

14718

14752

An engraved gold cigarette case with white champlevé enamel and a monogram in Cyrillic script — H — set with rose diamonds. Its working drawing (above) indicates the complexity of the work. It took no less than two months in 1917 for the Finnish master Jalmari Haikonen to engrave the case.

chance been preserved to our day. For the student of the goldsmith's art this small collection in its way offers an excellent insight into the working practices of the Wigström *atelier* (see p.25).

With its treasure-trove of decorative minerals from mines in Siberia, the Caucasus and the Urals, Russia provided Fabergé and his workmasters with hardstones which were cut, carved and polished at the lapidary works at Ekaterinburg in Siberia, at Peterhof outside St. Petersburg, and within the capital itself. A German lapidary master, Karl Woerffel, had set up his workshop there, and Fabergé began working with him and also with the lapidary Stern, based at Idar-Oberstein in Germany. The use of hardstones very soon became an important aspect of the production, and in order to ensure supplies of the highest quality Fabergé established his own lapidary workshops. These were headed by the workmaster Peter Mikhailovich Kremlev, who employed some twenty craftsmen in the years leading up to the First World War.[25] The importance of hardstones in Fabergé's production can be seen from a study of the objects made in Wigström's workshop between 1911 and 1916, which shows that well over thirty percent of the completed pieces included hardstones.

When the lapidaries had finished their work — to precise designs supplied by Fabergé's artists — mounters at the Wigström workshop finalized the objects by adding precious metal parts to the minerals.[26]

Another very important area in which Fabergé excelled, and a major concern and special interest of Carl Fabergé himself, was the art of enameling, which he developed with the help of the highly skilled craftsman Nikolai Alexandrovich Petrov.[27] Unlike the other workmasters, Petrov carried out the most demanding work himself, with the assistance of his brother Dmitri. The pressure on this

Another working drawing from the Wigström workshop, showing a Louis XV-style cigarette case in nephrite and chased gold.

A small hexagonal box with turquoise cover, the sides enameled white and overlaid with two-colored gold wreaths held by turquoises.

workshop, which soon became of central importance to Fabergé, must have been enormous, for of the objects made in Wigström's workshop from 1911 to 1916, every other piece was decorated with enamel. The exquisite quality of Petrov's enameling was the product not only of superb craftsmanship, but also of tremendous patience. In this painstaking process, the transparent enamel was applied on an engraved background in five to six layers, each one separately fired in the oven. How Petrov managed to meet the enormous demand for his work remains a mystery to this day.

Epilogue

The outbreak of the Great War in August 1914 was a tremendous blow to the House of Fabergé. A great many of its skilled workmen were sent to the front, leaving the workshops under-staffed: by 1915, the number of journeymen in the Wigström workshop had diminished from around sixty to twenty-eight.[28] Finally, in early 1918, the Bolsheviks closed the firm down. One of the workmen described his sense of loss: "The year 1918 begun, work had ceased all over, in factories and workshops. Private companies were not allowed. Our trade, the goldsmiths' trade, stopped as well and the stores were robbed. Fabergé, being such a big firm, left over 300 people out of work. The new leaders gave our directors the right to cash one and a half month's wages for each worker. I got three months' pay. A big sum of money. All of us at Wigström's were paid. And there we stood — speechless — with an ache in our hearts. We looked around us at the empty shop and it was like being at a funeral. It felt like having lost a dear relative. This was how I stopped working at Fabergé."[29]

For Henrik Wigström the loss of his workshop at first seemed inconceivable. Like many of his colleagues, he firmly believed that the nightmare

A circular gold locket with vertical black enamel stripes within rose *guilloché* enamel border, a basket of rose diamond flowers in the center.

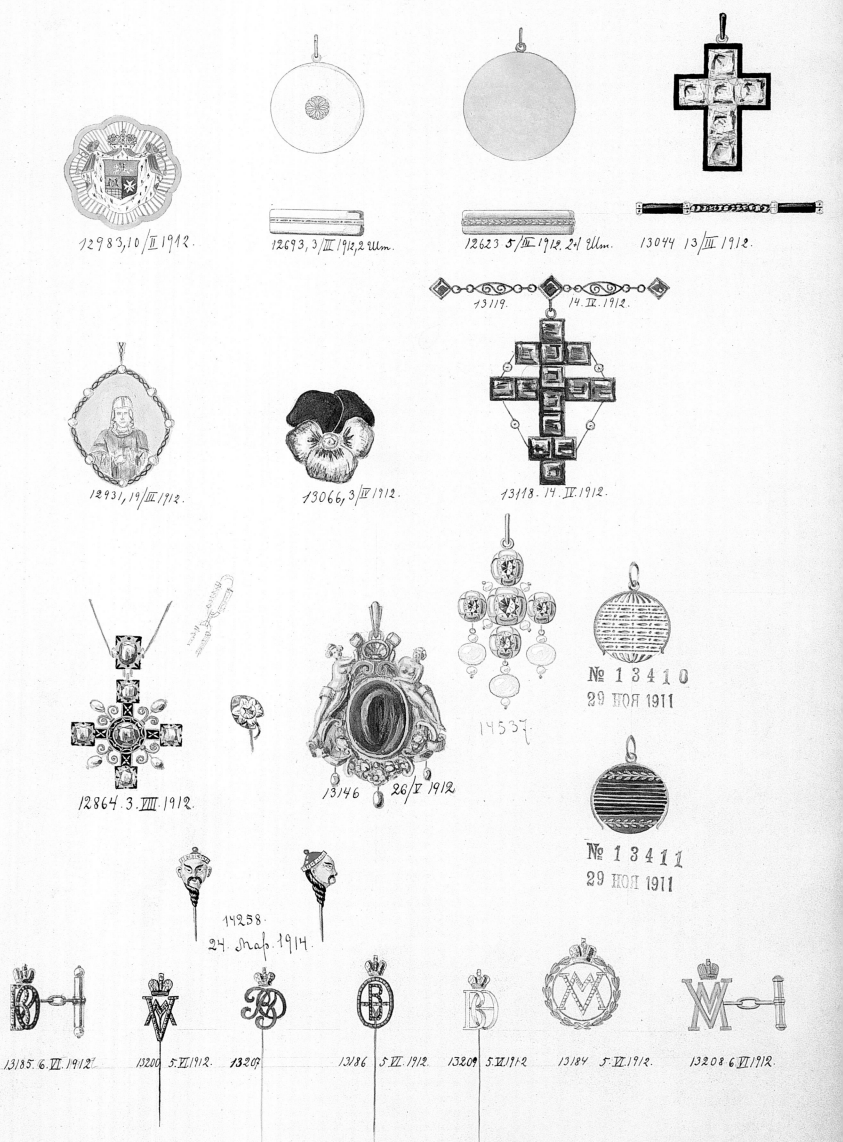

12983, 10/II 1912.

12693, 3/III 1912, 2 Шт.

12623 5/III 1912, 24 Шт.

13044 13/III 1912.

13119. 14.II.1912.

12931, 19/III 1912.

13066, 3/IV 1912.

13118. 14.IV.1912.

12864. 3.VIII.1912.

13146   26/V 1912.

14537

№ 13410
29 НОЯ 1911

№ 13411
29 НОЯ 1911

14258.
24. Мар. 1914.

13185. 6.VI.1912.   13200. 5.VI.1912.   13207.   13186. 5.VI.1912.   13209. 5.VI.1912.   13184. 5.VI.1912.   13208. 6.VI.1912.

PLATE *77*

Drawings of a variety
of jewels: crosses,
pendants, tie pins and
cufflinks. The bottom row
shows small presentation
pieces commissioned
by Grand Duchess Victoria
Feodorovna, known
also by her Christian name
Victoria Melita.

A side view of the hardstone
pirozhnik illustrated opposite,
another type of portrait
figurine similar to that shown
on plate 113.

Russia was going through in the years 1917-18 was of a temporary nature.
He decided to retreat for a while to his summer house, now on independent
Finnish territory.[30] But the situation was not a passing one, and the possi-
bility of return never came.

The remaining years of Henrik Wigström's life are described by his granddaughter, who spent her childhood summers in her grandfather's house:
"We children knew very well that our grandfather was a master goldsmith
and a most skillful one. The pounding beat of his chasing hammer was carried up to our rooms, late at night when we lay tucked up in our beds.
Grandpa sat at his workbench with its entire arsenal of tools, his bits and
pieces of material. We never found out if there were any concrete results
from this constant toiling. I have many a time, much later in life, stopped to
think about grandfather and his situation then and there. I now well understand why he so often shut himself up.

He, a successful and dynamic person, fifty-six years old, had to give up so
much — and without any warning: his career at Fabergé, his workshop, his
home in St. Petersburg and, last but not least, his not inconsiderable sav-
ings. He came across the border to his summer house in his native Finland.
He came there practically empty-handed. His daughter Lyyli, his efficient
workshop assistant, crossed the border, a bucket of seed-potatoes in one
hand and a bundle of sheet-music in the other. Wholly irrational, but symp-
tomatic of these Petersburgers! They could never envisage that the situation was to be permanent. They merely wanted to keep away from the
troubled city with its Bolshevik riots, waiting for the moment when they
could return to their daily routines."[31]

Five years later, in 1923, Fabergé's disillusioned chief
workmaster died, still at his house in the country.

Hardstone figurine of a
pie seller (*pirozhnik*) holding
a tray covered with
a cloth on his head, and
carrying another tray
in gold and yellow enamel.

The Wigström family
dacha (country house) at
Ollila, in Finland, not far
distant from St. Petersburg.
Henrik Wigström retired
here in 1918, following the
October Revolution
and the closure of the House
of Fabergé.

12700 20/X 1911

6 камн 12582 13/X 1911

№ 13408
25 ОКТ 1912

13068, 8/III 1912

6 кам. 12771 29/XI 1911

12696 28/IX 1911.

12766, 16/XII 1911, 2 шт.

12784 2/XII 1911.

12873 14/I 1912.

14388   14386   14387
22. Сенф. 1914.

13150 6.VII 1912.

Chapter Two

Patrons of Prestige
The Clientele of Fabergé

Caricature of Count
Mikhail Nikolaievich Grabbe
(1868-1942), aide-de-camp
to Emperor Nicholas II
from 1909, an elegant
aristocrat of *fin-de-siècle*
St. Petersburg.

The Wigström album contains a profusion of drawings of commissions,
purchases, and gifts relating to Fabergé's most eminent clients.

Jewelry — or for that matter any object in precious metal — might appear
lifeless without a provenance. Knowledge of the person to whom an object
originally belonged, of who commissioned it and why, lends it both added
interest and a sense of life. Of the almost one thousand objects illustrated
in the album, most were made between 1911 and 1913, either as specific
commissions or for stock. So far we have only fragmentary information
regarding Fabergé's clientele. The knowledge that we do have nonetheless
gives us a fairly clear idea as to who shopped at Fabergé and the purchases
they made.

Official commissions by the Emperor head the list. Next in importance
come private purchases by members of the Imperial family, followed by
those transacted by the Grand Dukes and Duchesses and their descendants.

In all, some one hundred thousand members of the Russian nobility lived in
St. Petersburg at the beginning of the twentieth century. There is no way of
knowing exactly how many of these frequented Fabergé, but clearly the
number was high. The élite among them — some two thousand families —
are listed in the *Almanach de St-Pétersbourg*. These were the highest-ranking
members of the establishment, who held
important posts and offices throughout the
Empire. The names of these august families
were also to be found among those invited to
court functions, to festivities at the Winter
Palace and to others held at the residences of
the Grand Dukes and Duchesses.

Fabergé's prestigious
clientele included Grand
Duke Sergei Alexandrovich
and his wife Elizaveta
Feodorovna, who lived
in the Beloselsky-Belozersky
Palace on Nevsky Prospekt.

PLATE 91

Drawings of rings,
pins, thimbles and a bracelet
with moss agate plaques.

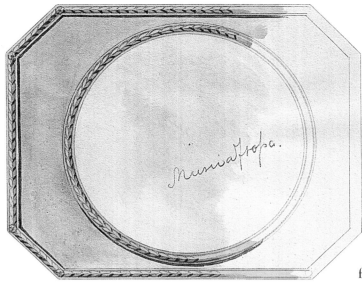

Drawing of a snuffbox
in pale blue enamel
on a *guilloché* ground,
with a miniature
in the center (Pl. 13).

The early twentieth century brought a new clientele to Fabergé, in the form of the rising class of financiers, industrialists, and businessmen.

Another significant group of clients came from the world of entertainment. The ballet dancers at the Imperial Mariinsky Theater, idolized by their public, famous singers, celebrated actors and actresses, and even gypsy artists are known to have been good customers.

The foreign clientele of Fabergé was particularly exalted. First and foremost it included the British Royal family and members of the numerous European monarchies, as well as of the various German principalities. Linked by bonds of kinship or friendship, members of this distinguished coterie were either recipients of gifts from their Russian relatives or customers in their own right. The Royal family of Siam also became an important client of the House of Fabergé. This came about as the result of a close friendship between the Russian Imperial family and the Royal House of Siam.[1]

In the wake of these many noble patrons, both the European and the American *beau monde* found their way to Fabergé. In these circles throughout the world, it became chic to own an object or jewel made by the renowned court jeweler of St. Petersburg.

The Emperor's official commissions

The Office of His Imperial Majesty administered the handling of the official gifts of the Empire. It was the custom for court suppliers to submit outlines and designs for gifts, from which the head of the Office

would make a preliminary selection. The Minister of the Court, who left the final decision on the design of important gifts to the Emperor, then approved this preliminary list.[2]

State gifts were carefully selected with the recipient's rank in mind, for like many other European countries, imperial Russia ranked people according to their position in society. Each title and post was listed in the Table of Ranks, first instituted by Peter the Great,[3] which contained separate tables for military and civil ranks. Thus the Emperor's official gifts may be divided into two categories: those for people of high rank and those for others of lesser rank. The most prominent category of objects consisted of lavish, gem-studded snuffboxes, decorated with a miniature portrait of the Emperor or the Imperial couple. Other gifts in the same category were rings, brooches and tie pins, also set with jeweled miniature portraits of the sovereign.

These luxurious gifts were presented to monarchs, to non-royal heads of state, and, very selectively, to other high-ranking personages at home and abroad. The occasions for such lavish gifts were state visits, coronations and other important occasions in the diplomatic calendar.[4] Plate 13 of the Wigström album features a presentation box bearing a profile of the Empress Alexandra Feodorovna (above).

During the reign of Nicholas II, the Office of His Imperial Majesty commissioned a total of 300 snuffboxes with the diamond-set cipher of the sovereign. These were intended as presentation pieces for prominent servants of heads of state,

The snuffbox corresponding to the drawing opposite, with a miniature portrait on porcelain of Empress Alexandra Feodorovna. This box served as a state gift, commissioned from Fabergé by the Office of His Imperial Majesty.

A photograph of Empress Alexandra Feodorovna, consort of Nicholas II, in full court dress, 1907. She wears a magnificent pearl and diamond tiara, one of the finest specimens of its kind, made in St. Petersburg by the court jeweler Bolin.

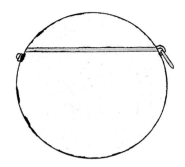

A match case (vesta case), and its corresponding drawing, in translucent white enamel on a *guilloché* ground. Marked with London import marks for 1910, it was purchased at the Fabergé London shop by Princess Cécile Murat on 9 December 1911 (Pl. 101).

including members of the cabinet, aides-de-camp, ambassadors and other prominent officials.[5]

A rarity in Fabergé's *œuvre* is a cigarette case, the modern version of the snuffbox, bearing the crowned cipher of the Emperor. Very few such pieces are known, though one example with a diamond-set "N II" is illustrated in the Wigström album (Pl. 141 - see p.64).[6] The recipient of this luxurious gift was General Alexander Sergeievich Lukomsky, of the General Staff, Chief of the Mobilization Department in 1911 and a figure of considerable importance.[7]

Cigarette cases decorated with a diamond-set crown or a double-headed eagle are some of the finest examples of imperial gifts of which the Emperor and his family made use on almost a daily basis. Wherever the Imperial family went or traveled, they met dignitaries who would receive elegant cigarette cases, as shown for example on plate 149 (below) of the album, as a souvenir of the memorable occasion.

In August 1914, a few days after the outbreak of the Great War, Dowager Empress Maria Feodorovna returned to Russia in great haste from a visit to her sister Queen Alexandra, traveling through Finland by train. As there was no time to prepare the imperial train for its august passenger, a crew of maintenance men under the young engineer Axel von Weissenberg accompanied her. Weissenberg did his utmost to make the trip as pleasant as possible, even to the point of decorating the Empress's salon. Lacking anything better, he filled it with large bouquets of elegant-looking weeds of the kind which grew in abundance along the rail track. The Empress responded to the young man's efforts by presenting him with a gold watch by

Drawing for a cigarette case decorated with a diamond-set double-headed eagle, an example of imperial gift (Pl. 149).

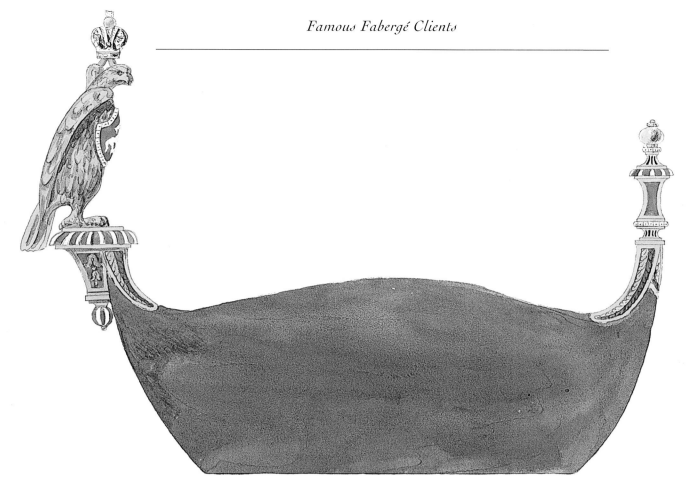

the Petersburg watchmaker Pavel Buhré, while Weissenberg's superior received a cigarette case by Fabergé decorated with the imperial crown.[8] Another traditional official gift or reward, customary since the reign of the Muscovite tsars of the sixteenth century, was the silver or silver-gilt *kovsh*. The early presentation *kovsh* was decorated with the double-headed eagle and engraved with the Tsar's name, the name of the recipient and the service rendered.[9] The tradition by which the Tsar presented a *kovsh* as a diplomatic gift or in gratitude for important services to the state was revived at the beginning of the twentieth century. The incentive for this was the renewed interest in Russia's past, which reached its peak in 1913 with the tercentenary celebrations of the Romanov dynasty. The leading Russian silver manufacturers produced impressive examples, as did Fabergé in Moscow.

In line with this development, Fabergé also created *kovshi* in decorative hardstone, especially in Siberian nephrite mounted with gem-studded symbols of the Empire: an example on plate 213 of the album shows a large nephrite *kovsh* with a crowned eagle perched at one end (above).

Drawing for a large nephrite *kovsh* with a crowned eagle at one end. Originally a drinking vessel, the *kovsh* became a customary imperial gift in the sixteenth century (Pl. 213).

A tapering bowenite match holder and its corresponding drawing (Pl. 101), the gold band enriched with green enamel, diamonds and sapphires.

The eagle wears the breastplate depicting St. George and the Dragon, the arms of Moscow. Another presentation *kovsh*, in the same expensive category (Pl. 263 - see p.121) features a handle in the shape of the imperial double-headed eagle, richly decorated with enamel, cabochon gemstones and rose diamonds. The nephrite dish with a handle in the form of a Russian eagle, on the same page, is a smaller version of a gift in the same category.

Official gifts to the clergy

The Emperor approved all ecclesiastical appointments in imperial Russia, and members of the clergy were presented with imperial awards in much the same way as meritorious members of the military or civilians. The album includes a richly jeweled pectoral cross (Pl. 79 - above) surmounted by an imperial crown set with cabochon sapphires and diamonds.

The cross was both a designation of office and an official recognition of long and unblemished service in the church. The equally richly jeweled episcopal panagia on the left-hand side of the same plate is depicted without its central holy image of the Mother of God, which would be painted by one of the miniaturists working for Fabergé.[10] Only bishops and metropolitans of the Russian Orthodox Church wore the panagia, which hung centrally on the breast from a chain.

A pectoral cross set with cabochon sapphires and diamonds (Pl. 79): an example of an official imperial gift to the clergy.

Semi-official commissions

The Office of His Imperial Majesty also handled commissions of a semi-official nature. These were gifts presented by the Imperial family at home and abroad for birthdays, christenings, weddings and anniversaries, and to members of their vast circle of family and friends.

Drawing of a badge (Pl. 79) commemorating the tercentenary of Romanov rule in Russia (1913).

The dossiers of His Imperial Majesty's Office record a large number of objects signed for by the Dowager Empress Maria Feodorovna before her frequent visits to Denmark, the country of her birth, and to England, to visit her sister Queen Alexandra.[11] When it came to personal gifts, the giver naturally took a closer interest in the choice, which was made from a variety of precious objects laid out in a special room at the Winter Palace. By invitation, court suppliers would leave suitable objects from their stock on approval in the hands of the administrators of the Office. A possible example of such personal gifts in the album is the miniature column (Pl. 165 - see p.76) surmounted by a double-headed eagle, intended for the display of a miniature portrait of a member of the Imperial family. Further examples are the miniature bust of Alexander III on the same plate (see p.76) and a selection of picture frames (Pl. 327, 329, 331 and 337). The royal collections of Britain and Denmark and those of the princely residences of Germany contain a profusion of these crowned frames, placed on tabletops and mantelpieces.

Another frame with the imperial crown, in the Louis XVI-style, shown on plate 327.

It is an interesting fact that in Russia, as connoisseurs of orders and medals are aware, the recipients of imperial orders, badges and mementoes frequently had copies made of them in a more precious metal, sometimes even set with valuable gemstones. Wigström also illustrates a breast badge commemorating the tercentenary of Romanov rule in Russia (Pl. 79 - opposite). The badges presented by the Emperor on the occasion of these festivities were manufactured in silver and silver gilt by the firm of Edvard Kortman,

Frames with the imperial crown, such as the oval enameled frame shown in this drawing, were another type of semi-official commission (Pl. 331).

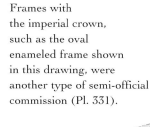

PLATE 103

Drawings of a match holder
and match cases in
a variety of colored enamels.

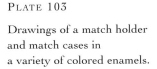

This match case was ordered
by Leopold de Rothschild
in his racing colors (Pl. 103);
it bears an inventory number
from Fabergé's London
branch, as well as English
hallmarks for 1911-12.

a specialist in the making of orders, medals, badges and *jetons*.[12] The example shown in the Wigström album, however, presumably belonged to a client who wished to have his prestigious badge remade by hand in gold and marked by Fabergé.

On 21 January 1913, the tercentenary was celebrated with a service in the Kazan Cathedral in St. Petersburg. The following day, the Emperor received delegations and their congratulations in the Winter Palace. All members of the imperial suite, officers of the Imperial Guard, members of the court, grand marshals and marshals of the nobility, ministers, viceroys, governors-general, governors, prefects, selected officers, administrators, diplomats, churchmen, representatives of the nobility, pages, lycée students, Pravoveds,[13] and others who offered their congratulations received this commemorative badge.[14]

Personal commissions by the Imperial family

The Easter eggs made by Fabergé for Alexander III and subsequently for Nicholas II were the most personal gifts from a devoted sovereign to his consort, the Empress.[15] These exquisite gifts for Easter morning epitomize the personal commissions of the Imperial family. Gifts within the family were all in their own way tokens of love: almost without exception they are linked to episodes or events in their own lives, as well as to important events in the history of Russia.

The Imperial Easter gift of the year 1912 from the Emperor Nicholas II to his mother, the Dowager Empress Maria, was an egg commemorating the centenary of the Russian victory over the armies of Napoleon in 1812, made of gold, enameled in green and decorated in the Empire style with double-headed eagles and trophies of war (Pl. 189 - see p.82).[16]

Gold and enamel match
case featuring opaque white
enamel bands and red and
green enamel borders (Pl. 103).

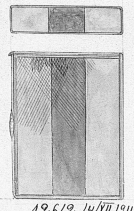

12612, 14/XII 1911
12889 20/III 1912.

12493 6/X 1911

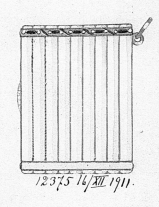

12765 25/XI 1911

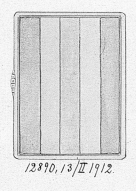

12375 16/XII 1911.

12890, 13/II 1912.

13019. 19.IV.1912.

13122 4/V 1912.

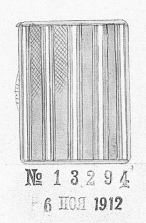

№ 13294
6 НОЯ 1912

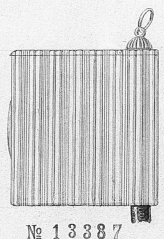
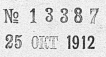

№ 13387
25 ОКТ 1912

№ 13386
25 ОКТ 1912

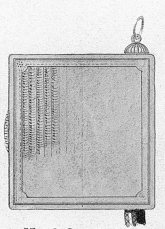

№ 13384
25 ОКТ 1912

№ 13385
29 ОКТ 1912

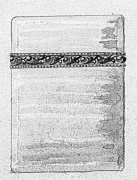

№ 13260
13 НОЯ 1912

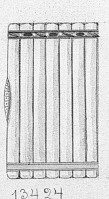

13424
8.XII.1912

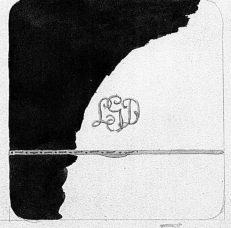

14089. 20. X. 1913

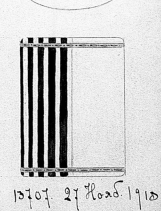

13707. 27 Нояб. 1913

12995 31/I 1912
25/IV 1912

PLATE 113

Drawing of a hardstone figurine representing Empress Alexandra Feodorovna's "Kamer-Kazak" (Chamber Cossack), or personal bodyguard, N.N. Pustinikov. The figurine was brought to America after 1925, but its whereabouts are presently unknown.

The Pavlovsk Palace State Museum possesses a hardstone figurine of A.A. Kudinov, Dowager Empress Maria Feodorovna's Kamer-Kazak from 1878. It is the second figurine referenced in the drawing on plate 113.

Examples of gifts alluding to the daily life of the Empresses are two statuettes of their Cossack bodyguards. A personal bodyguard chosen from the imperial escort, a Kamer-Kazak , accompanied both the Empress, Alexandra Feodorovna, and Dowager Empress Maria whenever they left the palace. The nature of their services earned these Cossacks the high regard of the Empresses, and must surely have prompted the Emperor to commission stone models of them from Fabergé.[17]

The statuettes are actual portraits, made from wax models by Fabergé's renowned sculptor Boris Frödman-Cluzel in the artist's studio.[18] The State Pavlovsk Palace Museum has in its collections the hardstone statuette of Andrei Alexeievich Kudinov (1852-1915), Dowager Empress Maria Feodorovna's Cossack guard. This faithful retainer had been the Dowager Empress's personal Chamber Cossack since 1878, eventually to die in his post in June 1915, presumably in Kiev, where the Dowager Empress had retired to escape the turmoil of wartime Petrograd. The high regard the Dowager Empress had for her faithful servant is borne out by information — albeit scanty — in the archives. When one of Kudinov's three daughters married, the Dowager Empress presented the young couple with generous gifts.[19]

The drawing on plate 113 (opposite), meanwhile, shows the Cossack Nikolai Nikolaievich Pustinikov (1857-1918), bodyguard to Empress Alexandra Feodorovna. He served the Empress from December 1894, soon after she had become the bride of the future Emperor, until 1st August

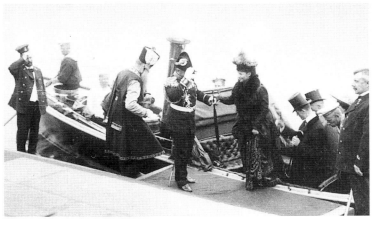

Both the Dowager Empress and the Empress had a Kamer-Kazak. Andrei Alexeievich Kudinov is shown here helping Dowager Empress Maria Feodorovna during one of her trips to Denmark.

Birds were a popular subject for hardstone figurines, here an owl in brown agate and a similar drawing (Pl. 111).

PLATE 121

Drawings of a variety
of cigarette cases,
one in rock crystal,
the others in varicolored
gold and enamel.

Drawing for a cigarette
holder in nephrite, gold and
enamel, from plate 161.

A gold-mounted amber
and blue *guilloché* enamel
cigarette holder, similar
to examples on plate 161.

1917, the fateful day when the Imperial family was imprisoned in Tobolsk. The portrait figure of the Cossack Pustinikov is known to have been kept at Pavlovsk until 1925[20] and was subsequently purchased by Armand Hammer and brought to New York. Its present whereabouts are unknown. As the dates below the drawing indicate, it served for both figurines, with different faces and beards.

The Grand Dukes and Grand Duchesses

The Grand Dukes and Grand Duchesses, their descendants and their relatives, the Romanovskis, Oldenburgs, and Mecklenburg-Strelitzes — all 51 of them — were without doubt most important *habitués* of Fabergé's showrooms.[21] On their sixteenth birthday, all male members of the Imperial family swore the oath of allegiance to the Emperor, and received the Order of St. Andrew and the First Class of all other Orders except the Order of St. George.[22] Each Grand Duke was expected to serve in the army or navy and to fulfill certain public obligations, serving on committees and actively supporting public charitable works as well as private ones. From his birth, a Russian Grand Duke was taught that *noblesse oblige* was not an abstract concept, but a living ideal.

As a member of the ruling house, each Grand Duke enjoyed an official status in imperial Russia which gave him not only obligations but also many privileges. The annual appanage of a Grand Duke during the reign of Nicholas II amounted to 200,000 roubles,[23] in addition to which each of them inherited sums from his parents, grandparents, and other relatives.[24] They also received occasional gifts of money from the sovereign and otherwise benefited from imperial generosity. At birth, funds and property

Drawing of a gold cigarette
case with green and
blue enamel decoration and
a diamond vase (Pl. 119)

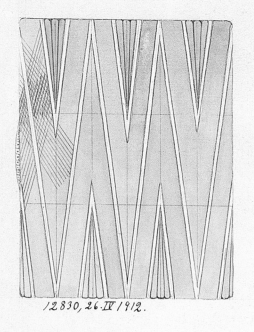

12830, 26. IV 1912.

13045 12. V. 1912.

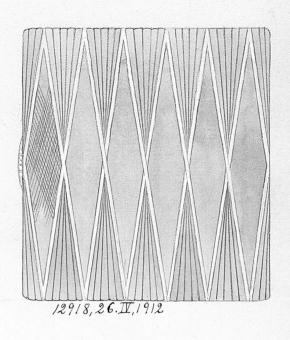

12918, 26. IV. 1912.

13077. 30. V. 1912

13102. 30. V. 1912.

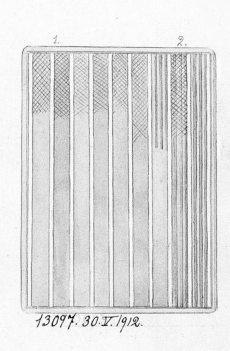

13097. 30. V. 1912.

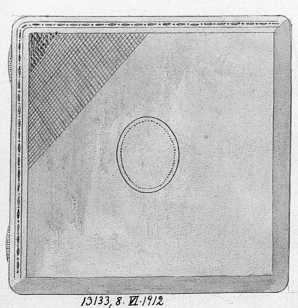

13133, 8. VI. 1912.

12919. 1. VI. 1912.

13121. 11. VI. 1912.

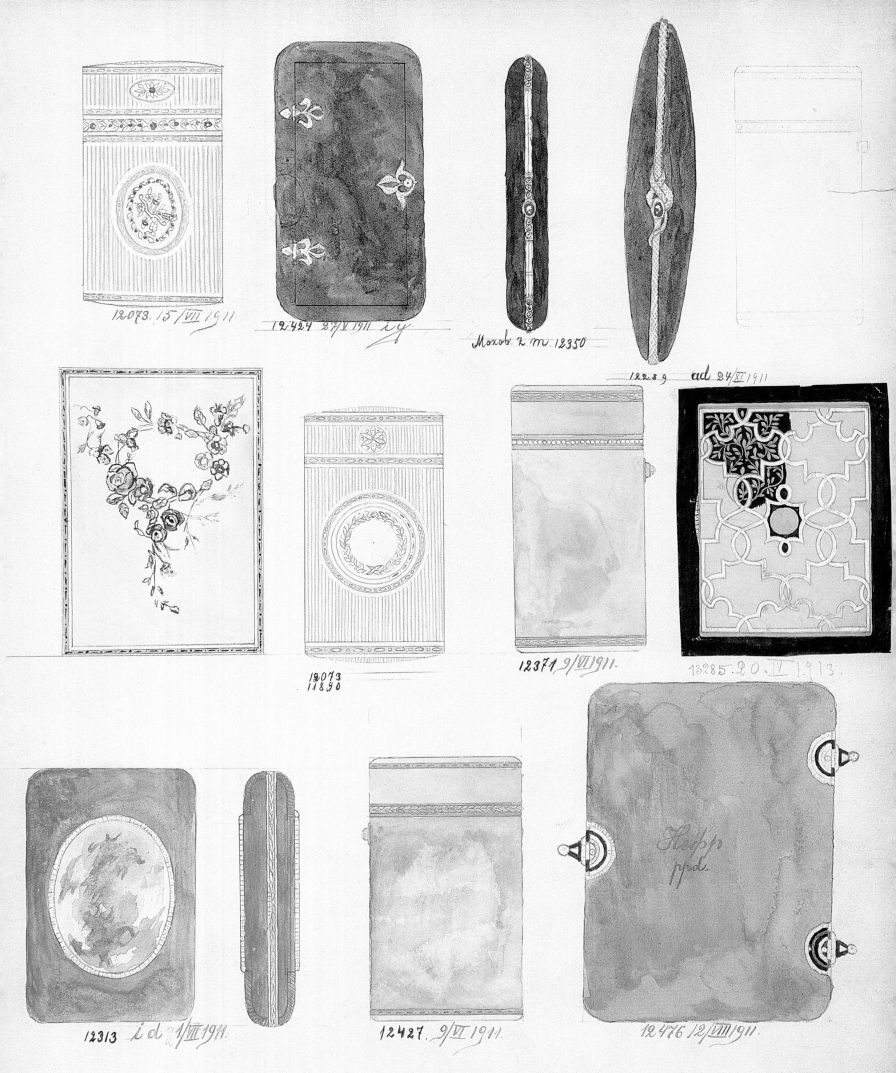

12073. 15/VII 1911.

12424 27/V 1911 ич

Мохов z m 12350

12289 ad 24/XI 1911

12073
11890

12371 9/VII 1911.

13285. 20.IV 1913.

12313 i d 1/VII 1911.

12427. 9/VI 1911.

Нефр рад.

12476 12/VIII 1911.

PLATE 129

Drawings of various
cigarette cases in
nephrite and enamel.

A signed photograph
of Grand Duchess
Victoria Feodorovna,
known as "Ducky",
and her husband
Grand Duke Kirill
Vladimirovich,
first cousin of Nicholas II.

were set aside for the new member of the family, and additional properties were purchased so that on reaching his majority at sixteen he would have a home in St. Petersburg and a house in the country, as well as his other residences. Each of the imperial princes also possessed an impressive library, significant works of art, and antiques and furnishings for his homes.[25]

Grand Dukes or their consorts were required to present gifts, very often of precious metal and bearing the crowned monogram of the donor, in recognition of services rendered. Numerous memoirs, biographies and letters of Russians living in exile bear witness to the variety and multiplicity of these gifts, as well as to the pleasure experienced by the recipients. The Wigström album depicts seven presentation pieces ordered by Grand Duchess Victoria Feodorovna, wife of Grand Duke Kirill Vladimirovich (Pl. *77* - see p.38)[26], and two of her presentation cigarette cases (Pl. 119 - below). These and the gold cufflinks and tie pins were completed by the workshop at the beginning of June 1912, either for a specific occasion or to be set aside until a suitable occasion arose. A few of the pieces bear the initials of the Grand Duchess in the Roman alphabet — V.M. for Victoria Melita — and were clearly intended as gifts for western Europeans.

A gift of a more personal nature may be found in a gold presentation box (Pl. 11 - overleaf), enameled in salmon pink and decorated with a central miniature portrait of a young boy set in a circle of rose diamonds. The years 1901 to 1911 and the name Dmitri — the facsimile of a signature by a child who has been taught correct penmanship — provide hints as to the provenance of this exquisite piece, the present whereabouts

Drawing of a cigarette
case commissioned
by Grand Duchess Victoria
Feodorovna, and bearing
her monogram in Cyrillic
script ВФ.

A cigarette case
in two shades of gold
and pink enamel
over a *guilloché* ground,
shown on plate 129.

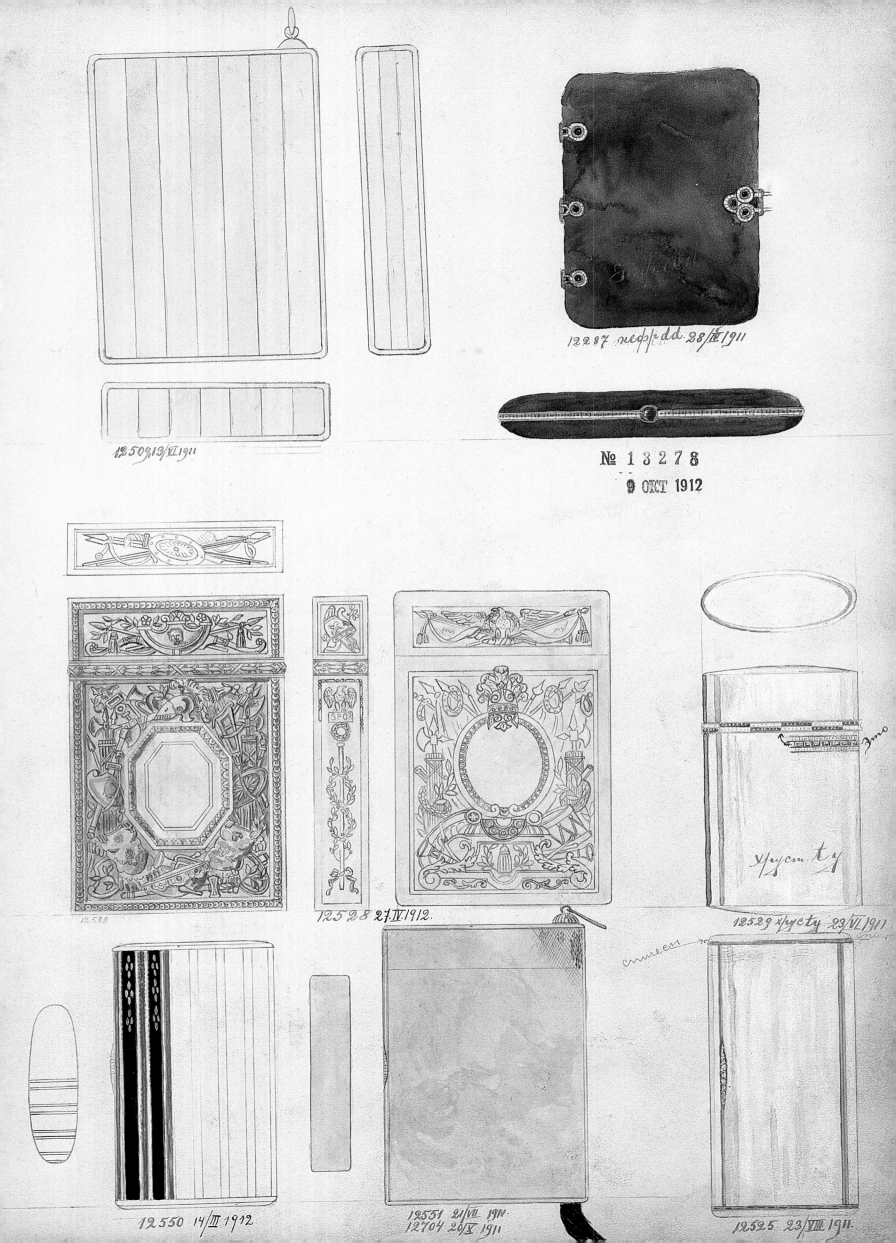

12509 13/VI 1911

12287 нефр dd 28/IX 1911

№ 13278
9 ОКТ 1912

12528 27/IV 1912

12529 хрусталу 23/VI 1911

12550 14/III 1912

12551 21/VII 1911
12704 20/X 1911

12525 23/VIII 1911

PLATE 131

Drawings of cigarette cases in rock crystal, nephrite, enamel, and gold.

of which are unknown. The box commemorates the tenth birthday of Prince Dmitri Alexandrovich, and was almost certainly presented by the boy's father, Grand Duke Alexander Mikhailovich, to his mother Grand Duchess Xenia Alexandrovna, the daughter of Alexander III. The young Prince Dmitri caught scarlet fever while the family was on a visit to Rome, and the resulting ear complications required surgical intervention, which was performed at Ai-Todor, the family estate in the Crimea. When the mastoid artery proved to be blocked, a specialist from Odessa was summoned. Having performed the operation, he stayed with the boy for several weeks at Grand Duke Alexander's insistence, until he was completely out of danger.[27]

Drawing of a box commemorating the tenth birthday of Prince Dmitri Alexandrovich (Pl. 11), probably presented to his mother by his father, Grand Duke Alexander Mikhailovich.

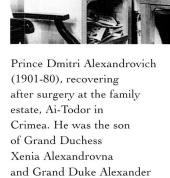

Prince Dmitri Alexandrovich (1901-80), recovering after surgery at the family estate, Ai-Todor in Crimea. He was the son of Grand Duchess Xenia Alexandrovna and Grand Duke Alexander Mikhailovich.

Another highly personal piece, unique in Fabergé's *œuvre*, is a lorgnette (Pl. 43 - see p.23) made for Grand Duchess Elizabeth (Elizaveta Feodorovna). The silver handle is covered with black enamel in a matte finish, with the crowned cipher of Grand Duchess Elizabeth, sister of Empress Alexandra Feodorovna and widow of Grand Duke Sergei Alexandrovich, who was assassinated in 1905. Rather austere in its simplicity, the lorgnette was made in September 1911, when Grand Duchess Elizabeth was already the Abbess of the Martha-Mary Convent, which she had founded in Moscow the previous year. Undoubtedly commissioned as a gift for her by a member of the Romanov family, this is perhaps the only monastic object ever made by Fabergé.[28]

A frame intended to display the photograph of a member of the Order of St. George is also included in the album (Pl. 315 - see p.136). This prestigious order, presented for bravery in battle, provided a productive "sideline" for

A rock crystal case with a gold mount set with rubies between diamond borders. It matches the second of the two options for the case shown on plate 131.

Grand Duke
Alexander Mikhailovich
and Grand Duchess
Xenia Alexandrovna,
daughter of Alexander III,
photographed in 1910
with their seven children.

the goldsmiths of the time. Objects decorated with the orange and black stripes of the Order formed exclusive gifts for the select circle of *honorés*. According to the sales ledgers of Fabergé's London branch, Grand Duke Michael (Mikhail Alexandrovich), younger brother of Nicholas II, purchased a frame with black and orange enameled stripes on silver in August 1911.[29] This could well be the frame depicted in Wigström's drawing, as it was completed shortly before the sale in London. Grand Duke Michael's wife, Countess Natalia Brasova, is also known to have commissioned a badge of St. George from Fabergé, made to order in 1915 and sent to her husband at the front.[30]

The love affair between Grand Duke Mikhail Alexandrovich and Mrs. Natalia Sergeievna Wulfert (later Countess Brasova) caused great concern in the Imperial family, who did everything in their power to bring the liaison to an end before it was too late. In the eyes of the Imperial family, Mrs. Wulfert was in all respects a most unsuitable person to marry Grand Duke Michael, who was second in order of succession to the throne. She was a commoner, she was twice divorced, and to crown it all she was well known for her independent political views. But Grand Duke Michael was deeply smitten with the beautiful Natasha, and nothing would persuade him to give her up. Escaping the members of the Security Police, the Okhrana, dispatched to tail them, the lovers succeeded in marrying secretly in Vienna. In a state of profound shock, the Dowager Empress wrote from Denmark to her eldest son, the Emperor, on

Grand Duke
Mikhail Alexandrovich,
Nicholas II's younger
brother, with his morganatic
wife Countess Brasova,
whom he married against
the will of the
Imperial family in 1912.

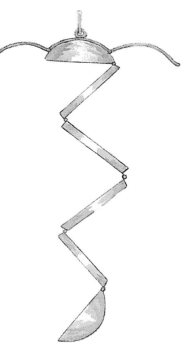

4 November 1912: "Now I must tell you about another terrible blow! I have just received a letter from Misha in which he announces that he has got married! It is unbelievable — I can hardly understand what I am writing — it is so appalling in every way that it nearly kills me! I beg only this one thing of you: that it be kept absolutely secret to avoid another scandal! There have been secret marriages in the past which one pretended to know nothing about."[31]

Drawing of a brooch in white *guilloché* enamel, with the crowned name "Serge", probably a gift from Grand Duke Sergei Mikhailovich (Pl. 75).

This disobedience to the Emperor resulted in the enforced exile from Russia of the newly-weds — a price the Grand Duke was willing to pay. And the marriage, based as it was on mutual respect and passionate love, was a most happy one. On the outbreak of the Great War, the Emperor was prepared to forgive his brother, and Grand Duke Michael was recalled to Russia to command the Caucasian Native Cavalry Division. When Nicholas II abdicated, he did so in favor of his brother Michael. The Grand Duke did not accept the throne and abdicated after one day as Emperor of Russia, on 3 March 1917.

The album contains a small brooch (Pl. 75 - left), presumably commissioned as a gift by Grand Duke Sergei Mikhailovich,[32] decorated in white *guilloché* enamel and bearing an imperial crown set with cabochon sapphires and diamonds. Grand Duke Sergei was one of the six members of the Romanov family murdered in Alapajevsk by the Bolsheviks. As a young man he and his brothers were often in the company of the Tsarevich, Nikolai Alexandrovich (the future Nicholas II). The love of his life was the celebrated ballerina Mathilda Kshesinskaia, but for many years he had to be content to admire her from afar.

From the day of her début in 1890 in the ballet troupe of the Imperial Theater, the delightful Kshesinskaia caught the eye of Alexander III. He

Drawings of a modernist spherical locket pendant (Pl. 75). Thanks to an ingenious mechanism, it unfolds to reveal hinged compartments for photographs.

12702. 20/X 1911.

Орлеъбіd

12581 2gаñ 28/X 1911.

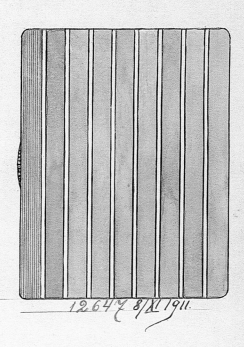

12647 8/XI 1911.

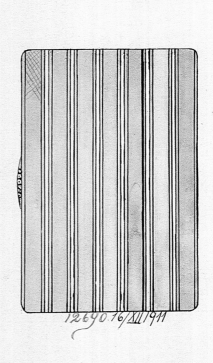

12690. 16/XII 1911.

4 12365 3/X 1911
12759 10/II 1912

12364 27/VI 1911.
2 шт. 11. IV 1912. 1 шт. 13. IV. 1912.
1 шт. 13229. 9. VII. 1912. 1 шт. 18. VII 1912.

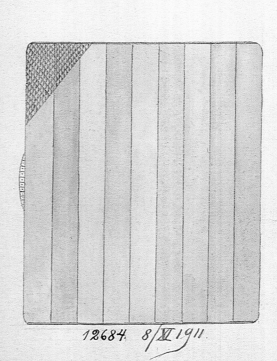

12684. 8/VI 1911.

12149 22/XI 1911

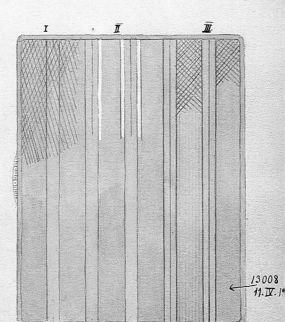

13008
11. IV. 1

I 12683 27/X 1911. III 12727. 23/XI
Двѣ штуки. II 12758 23/XII 1911

PLATE 139

Drawings of cigarette
cases in varicolored gold,
hardstone and enamel, most
versions created in 1911.

arranged for a liaison between his young and inex-
perienced son, the Tsarevich Nikolai and the young
ballerina, without the knowledge of the Empress.
The ballerina's memoirs give the impression that the
romance that developed between the Tsarevich and
herself — their very first true love — left them both

A box showing the
exquisite craftsmanship of
Wigström's goldsmiths, here
combining enameling, gold
chasing and a miniature
enamel painting of Falconet's
statue of Peter the Great.

with a flame that was never completely extinguished. Both, however, knew
from the start that the future Emperor would one day marry a princess of
the blood. When the romance came to its inevitable end, Grand Duke
Sergei Mikhailovich was there to dry the ballerina's tears. He too was
deeply smitten with her, and retained very warm feelings towards her to the
end of his life. When the ballerina gave birth to a son, Vladimir, in 1903, he
was convinced that the child was his — though another admirer, Grand
Duke Andrei Vladimirovich, was later to marry her.

Two mementoes of Grand Duke Sergei's love for Kshesinskaia were found
in his uniform pocket after his body was recovered in Alapajevsk. One was
a small gold locket set with an emerald and containing the ballerina's photograph and the inscription "Mala", Mathilda's pet name; the other was a
small gold pendant in the shape of a potato. When the exiled Grand
Duchess Xenia Alexandrovna gave Mathilda Kshesinskaia these two
pieces, the ballerina omitted to tell her that the motif of the pendant
referred to the "Potato Club", formed by the young bachelor Grand Dukes
and their aristocratic friends with the sole aim of fostering intimate
associations with ladies of the *demi-monde*.[33]

A gold barrette commissioned for or by Prince Gavriil
Konstantinovich, presumably for his twenty-fifth
birthday on 15 July 1912 (Pl. 91 - see p.40),

A cigarette case
in two shades
of gold — red and
green — similar
to the lower right-hand
drawing on plate 139.

Two drawings (front and back) of a match case, with the monogram of Grand Duke Andrei Vladimirovich and the symbol of the Russian artillery under Alexander I and Nicholas I (Pl. 107).

bears his crowned monogram. The second son of the literary Grand Duke Konstantin Konstantinovich, Prince Gavriil, like so many of his close relatives in the Romanov family, met and fell in love with a woman he could not marry owing to his position — in his case the ballet dancer Antonina Nesterovskaia, whom he had met at Mathilda Kshesinskaia's house in 1911. Prince Gavriil was finally able to marry his enduring love only after the Revolution.

A small match case (Pl. 107 - left) was a gift to Grand Duke Andrei Vladimirovich for his thirty-seventh birthday on 2 May 1916. It bears the crowned monogram of the Grand Duke on one side and the Russian imperial double-headed eagle on the other. The eagle, with lowered wings and grasping in its claws a pair of crossed cannon, was the symbol of the Russian artillery during the reigns of Alexander I and Nicholas I. As we have seen, Grand Duke Andrei was the future husband of the ballerina Mathilda Kshesinskaia, whom he met at the height of her career, when she was twenty-seven and he only twenty. A son, Vladimir, was born to the couple, but they were unable to marry until 1921, by which time they were living in exile after the Revolution, and Vladimir was eighteen.

A large gold cigarette case (Pl. 145 - right) was a gift to Prince Ioann Konstantinovich for his twenty-fifth birthday, on 5 July 1911. With his brother Konstantin and his father's cousin Grand Duke Sergei, Prince Ioann was murdered at Alapajevsk in 1918. He was married to Princess Helen, the daughter of King Peter I of Serbia,

Drawing of a gold cigarette case with a décor in the Louis XV style (Pl. 145), bearing Prince Ioann Konstantinovich's crowned monogram.

who adopted the Russian name Elena Petrovna. Her monogram appears in the album on an enameled background and with garlands of roses, set on a beautiful miniature easel (Pl. 325 - below).

The Russian aristocracy

Members of the aristocracy formed the backbone of Fabergé's clientele. As Franz Birbaum, head designer at the House of Fabergé, recalled: "All the aristocracy of St. Petersburg, persons of title, rank and wealth, could be seen there every afternoon between four and five o'clock, and the shop was particularly crowded during Holy Week, when everybody rushed to buy the traditional Easter eggs…"[34] Fabergé's shop was the perfect spot in which to be seen and to see for oneself.

Numerous and affluent, with a tremendous appetite for jewels and objets d'art, the aristocracy was in reality the guarantor of the firm's success. Most of the pieces illustrated in the Wigström album were in all probability commissions or purchases by members of this important group of customers. Many of Wigström's drawings bear the monograms of the intended owners, often surmounted by coronets, but, with only a few exceptions, ascertaining the identity of the people behind these initials is no easy task today. The coat of arms of the Galitzin family is recognizable in the colorful brooch or *jeton* on plate 77, while the necklace on plate 75 includes the coat of arms shared by four families listed in the *Gerbovnik*: Podolsky, Rachinsky, Sakhnovsky and Tikhotsky.[35]

In the turmoil of 1917 and the following decades, the collections of the Russian aristocracy were dispersed, and regrettably most of the pieces they contained lost their provenance.

Drawing of a miniature easel
with the monogram of Princess
Elena Petrovna (Pl. 325).

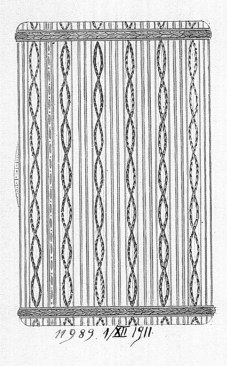

11989. 1/XII 1911.

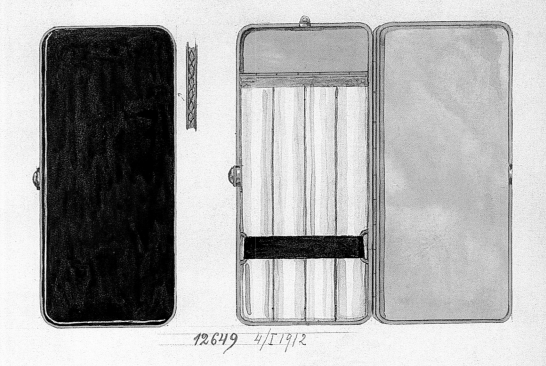

12649 4/I 1912

12756, 25/XI 1911

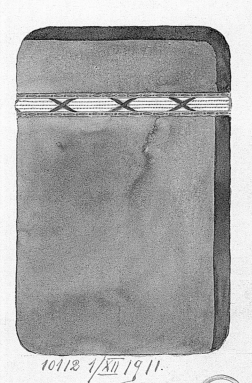

10112 1/XII 1911.

12747, 23/XII 1911.

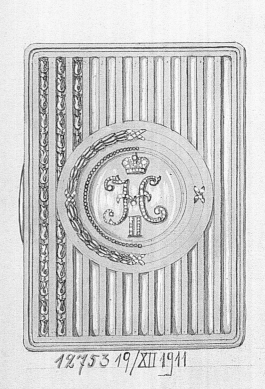

12753 19/XII 1911

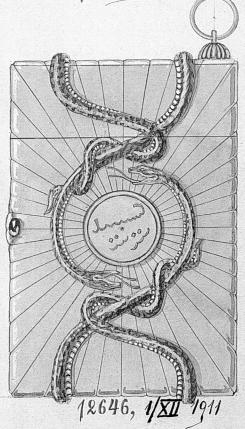

12646, 1/XII 1911

12892. 20/IV 1912.

PLATE 141

Drawings of various
cigarette cases in enamel,
nephrite and varicolored
gold, among them
a presentation case bearing
the monogram of Nicholas II.

A cigarette case in polished
gold with intertwined
snakes in platinum, a New
Year's gift from Princess
Cécile Murat to M. Charles
Luzarche d'Azay in 1912,
shown on plate 141.

In Fabergé's heyday, the St. Petersburg season, which
lasted from September until Lent, was one never-ending
round of court festivities, receptions, banquets, gala
performances at the imperial theaters, and costume and
fancy balls in the capital's palaces and hôtels parti-
culiers. Noble families such as the Sheremetevs, the
Voeikovs, the Kleinmichels, the Orlovs, the Narishkins,
and the Galitzins vied with each other to host the most elegant and talked-
about dinners and dances with the wittiest theme. Countess Elizabeth
"Betsy" Shuvalov, *née* Princess Bariatinsky, was one of the most famous
hostesses of *fin-de-siècle* St. Petersburg. Her "Black and White Ball" and
"Colored Wigs Ball", both held in 1914, achieved legendary status, and
numerous biographies and photographs bear witness to the unforgettable
soirées held in her elegant residence on the Fontanka Embankment —
events which were of course the perfect occasion to show off the latest
jewelry.

Members of the Yusupov family were undoubtedly among Fabergé's most
important customers. In 1907, the workshops created a spectacular table
clock in the shape of an Easter egg, commemorating the twenty-fifth wedding anniversary of Princess Zenaïda Yusupova and her husband Prince
Felix Yusupov, Count Sumarokov-Elston, who took his wife's name by
imperial dispensation. Numerous pieces by the court jeweler adorned the
many residences of the Yusupovs, and some have been preserved to this
day.[36] But, as noted by Birbaum in his memoirs, many wealthy Russians
also made substantial purchases of jewelry abroad.[37] A glimpse of
the contents of the jewel-box of Princess Zenaïda and that of
her daughter-in-law, Princess Irina Alexandrovna, reveals

A nephrite cigarette case
with a gold mount enameled
in white and set with rubies.
It is similar to an example
shown on plate 141.

Leopold de Rothschild purchased this cigarette case with his family's racing colors (illustrated on plate 141 - see p.64) from Fabergé's London branch in 1911.

that the famous Houses of Cartier and Chaumet made much of the princesses' jewelry in Paris. However, the spectacular purchase from France of the largest pearl in the world, once worn by Empress Eugénie, was entrusted to the skilled hands of Carl Fabergé, who also designed a modern setting for it.[38]

Only one small object among all the Yusupov commissions has so far been found in the Wigström album. This is the gold wedding *jeton* (below) made for the younger generation: Prince Felix Felixovich and his bride Princess Irina Alexandrovna, the Emperor's cousin. Literally the whole of Russian high society was invited to their sumptuous wedding on 9 February 1914, which was the last really great social event in the country before the outbreak of war.

Wealthy industrialists

The early years of the twentieth century witnessed a dynamic growth in industry in the St. Petersburg area, particularly in the engineering field. The Putilov works, a large-scale metalworking factory employing thousands of workers, was the largest industrial entrepreneur in the region. The founder of the company was the metallurgist I.N. Putilov, who became a notable figure in financial circles.

When the rouble was put on the gold standard in 1897, there was a substantial influx of foreign businesses into Russia. The new economic climate proved an incentive to investment by European and American entrepreneurs, who had already been attracted by the cheap labor available in Russia.[39]

The enormously successful rubber-processing company, "The Russian-American India Rubber Co", known in Russia by its trade name

The Wigström album contains a sketch (Pl. 79) and loose prints of the gold wedding *jeton* of Prince Felix Yussupov and his bride Princess Irina Alexandrovna.

On 9 February 1914,
Prince Felix Yusupov
married the Emperor's
cousin, Princess
Irina Alexandrovna,
who epitomized Russian
beauty and elegance.

The Yusupov wedding
jeton delivered by Fabergé
shows on either side
the white enamel crowned
monogram of the bride
— ИА — and groom
— ФЮСЗ — in Cyrillic
script, together with the
wedding date.

"Treugolnik", soon became the world's largest manufacturer of rubber galoshes. The sole sales rights were held by the Swiss businessman Leopold Neuscheller, whose two adopted sons, Max Othmar-Neuscheller and the Dutchman Hindrik van Gilse van der Pals, directed the "Trading House Neuscheller" in its second generation, expanding its sales beyond the borders of Russia. In the wake of their business successes both families became important members of the *haute bourgeoisie* of St. Petersburg. Their luxurious homes became the setting for sumptuous dinner parties and dances, and their lifestyles and interiors decorations were featured in the fashionable journal *Stolitsa i Usadba* (Town and Country). Both the Neuschellers and the van Gilse van der Pals were important customers of Fabergé.[40]

Over the eighty years in which it operated in Russia, the Swedish Nobel family created one of the world's largest industrial concerns, embracing companies in oil and chemicals, railways and shipping, engineering and munitions. In all, the Nobel companies in Russia employed almost 50,000 workers in the years up to 1917.[41]

This new and enormously successful group of industrialists became important clients of Russian goldsmiths, both through their businesses and as private individuals. The goldsmiths, for their part, were delighted, as Birbaum recalls: "I must say that it was incomparably easier and more pleasant to work with them [the industrialists]: nearly all of them were gifted with practical good sense, had no pretensions to artistic initiative and did not impose their ideas and designs. They rightly assumed that a designer was a specialist on the same level as an engineer or a bookkeeper, and that any directive could only be harmful. When ordering a present, they very often did not even define any kind of article, but only specified its maximum

Drawing of a *guilloché*
enameled table lighter with
a nephrite base (Pl. 105).

A nephrite cigarette case with a gold an enamel mount. It was completed on 29 May 1912 (Pl. 147).

PLATE 147

Drawings of jeweled cigarette cases, three of which are carved in nephrite.

price, the intended recipient and the occasion of the presentation. In these circumstances, the artist could work without any limitations on his creativity, which is important, and could feel that he bore full responsibility for his creations, which is no less important."[42]

The industrialists created their own set of prerequisites, which included the provision of important gifts to their customers at home and abroad. These company gifts were for the most part produced by the goldsmiths.

The practice adopted by the Nobel family serves as a good example. Emanuel Nobel, head of Nobel Brothers at the turn of the century, placed important orders with Fabergé on a continuous basis for over twenty years, both through his companies and as a private individual. The Nobel company orders consisted of the whole range of goldsmiths' products, from large objects to small items of jewelry, including both custom-made and mass-produced articles. The rapidly increasing output of the Baku oil fields in the Caspian Sea provided the motivation for costly company gifts and rewards. Examples of mass-produced but nevertheless expensive gifts included gold and silver plaques and medals, which were presented by the hundreds to employees and customers. Thousands of gold and silver *jetons*, or commemorative badges intended as gifts, were also produced.

Custom-made items, meanwhile, included specially designed and hand-made jewelry for the wives of employees and clients. As Birbaum relates, Nobel was not only a generous client but also a discerning one: "One of the oil magnates [Emanuel Nobel] was famous for his lavish gifts — indeed, giving them sometimes seemed to be his sole occupation and pleasure. Several of his orders were always in the process of execution in our work-

A nephrite cigarette case with diamond set hinges and thumbpiece, shown on plate 147.

12735 29.V.1912.

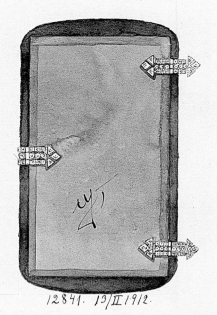

12841. 13/II 1912.

12898,13/II 1912

12977 9/II 1912

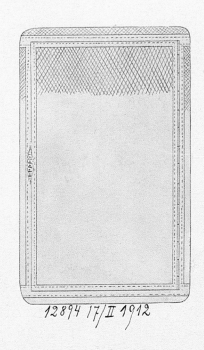

12894 17/II 1912

12884. 22/II 1912

12880, 25/II 1912

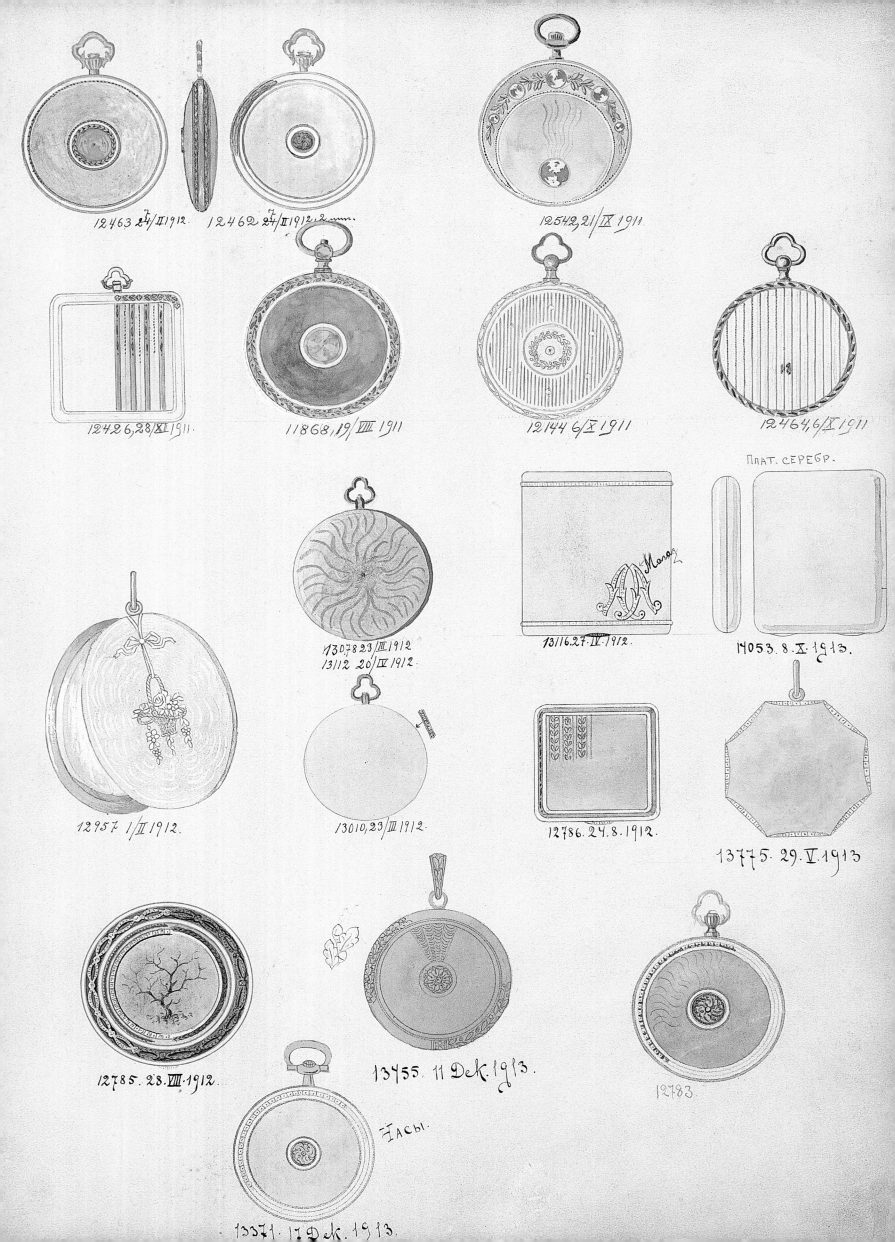

12463 24/II 1912.

12462 27/II 1912, 2 mm.

12542, 21/IX 1911.

12426, 28/XI 1911.

11868, 19/VIII 1911

12144 6/X 1911

12464, 6/X 1911

ПЛАТ. СЕРЕБР.

13078 23/III 1912
13112 20/IV 1912.

13/16.27.IV.1912.

14053. 8.X.1913.

12957 1/II 1912.

13010, 23/III 1912.

12786. 24.8.1912.

13775. 29.V.1913

12785. 28.VIII.1912.

13455. 11 Дк. 1913.

12783

Часы.

13371. 11 Дк. 1913.

A compact in gold with white enamel stripes, completed in Wigström's workshop in October 1911 (Pl. 151).

shops, and he came to look at them from time to time. Very often a present found its destination only after it was finished, and when the workshops were closed, some of his orders remained incomplete... Emanuel Nobel was a great admirer of the goldsmith's art and had a special predilection for enamels: some of his orders were for extremely large articles in painted enamels on gold. A series of small pieces of jewelry in rock crystal with frost-like patterns in tiny brilliants was also interesting."[43]

These small items of jewelry in rock crystal and diamonds were designed by the young Finnish artist Alma Pihl, who was the junior designer at the workshop of her uncle Albert Holmström, head of the Fabergé jewelry workshop. Two of her designs are included in the Wigström album (Pl. 73 - see p.124).[44]

Varvara Bazanova, the young heiress to the Bazanov family fortune, founded on gold and platinum mines, railways and shipping companies, married the aristocrat Alexander Kelch. The couple then proceeded to vie with the Imperial family in the lavishness of their lifestyle, commissioning a series of opulent Easter eggs from Fabergé, and acquiring a magnificent collection of gemstones and an extraordinary silver service made specially for the Gothic dining room of their palatial home in St. Petersburg.[45]

Fabergé and the stars of the stage

All Carl Fabergé's close associates agree on the importance of his customers from the world of entertainment. As Franz Birbaum bluntly remarked: "We cannot pass by in silence the most profitable clientele which, as anybody can guess, was the demi-monde, from ballet dancers to gypsies and down..." The same observation was more elegantly expressed by Henry C. Bainbridge: "What of the ballerinas, those queens of graceful

A pocket watch in opalescent enamel over a *guilloché* ground, similar to examples shown on plate 151.

A sliding locket revealing three compartments for photographs. It is enameled with a dendritic motif on a *guilloché* ground (Pl. 151).

PLATE 151

Drawings of fob watches, lockets and compacts in various shades of enamel.

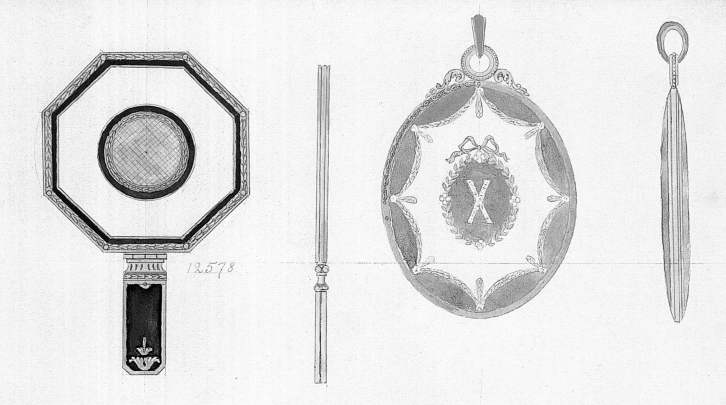

12578 15/III 1912.   12556. здано 5/VIII 1911

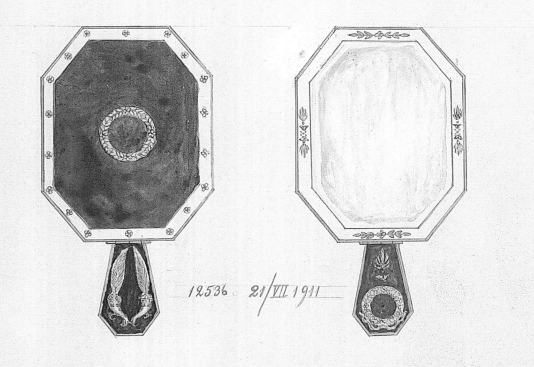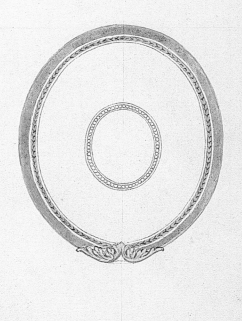

12536   21/VII 1911

12577

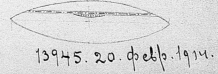

12543 6/X 1911   13945. 20. февр. 1914.

PLATE 153

Drawings of hand mirrors,
a sliding locket with
a mirror and a pill box.

Mauve enamel cushion-
shaped bonbonnière
with enamel roses and
foliage in relief and a rose
diamond ribbon.

movement and self-expression, themselves consummate emblems in flesh
and blood, whose art gave them rank but little below that of the Imperial
family — Ksheshinskaia [sic] and her Fabergé collection; Preobrajenskaia;
Pavlova; Lopokova; and Karsavina and her mascot brooch, a wonderful
Siberian amethyst, the finest of a set presented to Count Zuboff by
Catherine the Great and set with a surround of single brilliants by Fabergé
... and Balletta of another art, but what matter, and her Fabergé smoky
rock crystal goblet of surpassing beauty ... and perhaps the most beautiful
thing Fabergé ever made; and Cavalieri, of still another art, and her
Fabergé gold cup for Traviata."[46]

St. Petersburg boasted three opera houses, a famous ballet company, a
lively operetta season and several opulent theaters catering for every taste,
from the respectable, imperial-subsidized Alexandrinsky which staged seri-
ous plays, to the frivolous Nevsky Farce. Attending these theatrical events,
premieres and frequent benefit performances was very much a part of life
for the Imperial family, its entourage, courtiers and the entire *beau monde*.
Gifted artists were admired by all, and idolized by many.

The home of the Russian Imperial Ballet, the Imperial Mariinsky Theater,
staged ballet performances on Wednesdays and Sundays. On those nights
the balletomanes of St. Petersburg filled the 2,000-seat auditorium to
capacity. Many of the ballerinas became favorites of the members of the
Imperial family, foremost among them being Mathilda Kshesinskaia, as has
already been seen. The reigning ballerina of the Mariinsky Theater in the
last decade of the nineteenth century and the first of the twentieth, she was
the only Russian artist to be awarded the official title *Prima ballerina asso-
luta*, and was celebrated for her vivacity and glamor, as well as for the bril-
liance of her gypsy roles. When her romance with the future Emperor

The drawing of
the bonbonnière opposite,
taken from plate 159.

A small circular *guilloché*
gold box featuring
concentric white enamel
bands (Pl. 157).

A carved rhodonite parasol handle in the form of a horse's head over a white *guilloché* enamel collar.

Nicholas II ended, she was consoled by two Grand Dukes, Sergei Mikhailovich and Andrei Vladimirovich, marrying the latter after the Revolution.

Throughout her career, Kshesinskaia was showered with jewels, many of them specially commissioned from Fabergé. In 1911, to celebrate her twentieth anniversary as a performing ballerina, she received an official imperial gift of a platinum eagle set with diamonds. Her devotee Grand Duke Sergei went back stage on behalf of the Emperor to request that she wear the diamond eagle that night. This she did, dancing the *pas-de-deux* in Paquita. Grand Duke Sergei's own gift to her was a mahogany box containing a collection of canary yellow diamonds to be mounted in jewelry of her own choosing. From Grand Duke Andrei, meanwhile, she received a diamond and sapphire tiara in the Egyptian style, designed for the ballet *The Pharaoh's Daughter.*[47]

A cane handle featuring a lapis lazuli knob with a gold and white enamel collar bordered by diamonds (see a similar one on plate 63).

Another favorite was the French actress Mlle Elisabeth "Elisa" Balletta, who from 1891 to 1905 was on contract to the Mikhailovsky Theater, the venue for French and Russian drama and comedy. Mlle Balletta was more celebrated for her beauty than for her talent, and posterity has preserved few traces of her artistic career. Only two of her roles, both of minor significance, are known: Mme Leturc in *Les Trois Epiciers* and Cornaline in *Cendrillonnette*. In her person, however, she was truly impressive, with eyes that sparkled like diamonds, a mane of thick curly hair and the narrowest waist in the world. No wonder, then, that she caught the eye of Grand Duke Alexei Alexandrovich, known for his excellent taste.[48] His cousin, Grand Duke Alexander Mikhailovich, described him as "a case of fast women and slow ships": a barbed

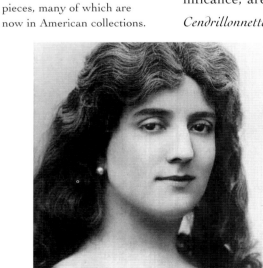

The French-born actress Elisa Balletta was an avid collector of Fabergé pieces, many of which are now in American collections.

reference to his responsibility as General-Admiral for the catastrophic defeat of the Russian fleet in the Russo-Japanese War of 1904-5. The lavish gifts purchased by the Grand Duke from Fabergé and bestowed on Mlle Balletta, especially during the war, caused a tremendous scandal and public outcry. In November 1904, Maxim Gorky wrote to his wife Ekaterina Peshkova: "Yesterday at the Mish [Mikhailovsky Theatre] someone in the front stalls loudly remarked on Balletta's entry [she was literally covered in diamonds]: 'Aha! This is where we find our Fleet! This woman wears a battleship on each finger!' The audacious outburst caused a fracas in the audience during which the police tried to eject the rowdy patriot, but the spectators gave him their vocal support. In the end it was the patriot who stayed and Grand Duke Alexei who thought it best to leave. The affair between Mlle Balletta and the Grand Duke became a *bête noire* among the general public. Satirical articles, mockery and scorn dogged the couple, and Mlle Balletta complained that she was being booed off stage. In 1905, pleading ill health, she applied for permission to cut short her contract with the theater. The Court Minister Freederickz gave his official consent, and Mlle Balletta paid the fine for her breach of contract and returned to her native Paris, where she lived to a ripe old age, dying only in 1959.

Known as the Queen of the Gramophone, Anastasia Vialtseva was the epitome of the beautiful artist showered with gifts of expensive jewelry by wealthy admirers.

Another Fabergé client, Mademoiselle Cavalieri was a dazzling Italian soprano.

Elisabeth Balletta was the owner of a truly exquisite collection of Fabergé masterpieces, including personal jewels, jeweled boxes, objects of fantasy and a miniature menagerie, for she was an ardent collector of animal figurines in various hardstones.[49] Many of these pieces are today in private hands, mainly in American collections.

The Italian soprano Natalina "Lina" Cavalieri (1874-1944)[50], another dazzling beauty, gave performances at concert halls in St. Petersburg between 1901 and 1912, singing the leading roles in all the famous operas, from *Traviata*, *Manon*, and *Faust* to *Carmen*, *La Bohême* and *Thaïs*. She became one of the most celebrated and admired artists of her day, and when her career in Russia was at its zenith, her portrait adorned postcards and chocolate boxes.

Mlle Cavalieri originally found her way to Russia with the help of Prince Alexander Bariatinsky, the scion of a well-known, esteemed, and wealthy aristocratic family, with whom she had an enduring love affair. He followed her on her performances abroad, in America and Europe, and lavished gifts upon her. In her role portraits, Cavalieri is pictured wearing the most sumptuous jewelry, including a tiara and a fantastic emerald necklace said to have been part of the Bariatinsky family jewels. Not merely the recipient of jeweled gifts, Mlle Cavalieri was also a client in her own right both at Fabergé and at Cartier.[51]

Anastasia Dmitrievna Vialtseva (1871-1913) was a celebrated mezzo-soprano in the popular genre, who performed in operettas and operas, and was especially loved for her interpretations of gypsy songs, which she performed all over Russia. Her life was a classic rags-to-riches success story, demonstrating how the daughter of a poor forester could, through hard work, gain fame and fortune. She married the dashing Colonel, later General, V.V. Biskupsky, and toured Russia in her own opulently furnished train car, matched only by those of the Imperial family. Her name appeared in the headlines of all the leading newspapers, above articles describing her fabulous jewels and her incredible fees. Known as the "Queen of the Gramophone", she produced over a hundred recordings between 1900 and

Smoky quartz bust
of Alexander III
on a cylindrical nephrite
column, bearing
the diamond-set cipher
of the Emperor (Pl. 165).

A two-color gold column
surmounted by the
Russian imperial eagle.
It holds a miniature
of Emperor Nicholas II who
presented it to Count
Eilenburg in 1909 (Pl. 165).

PLATE 165

Drawings of *objets
de vitrine*, the two pieces
shown on this page
and a miniature toilet table.

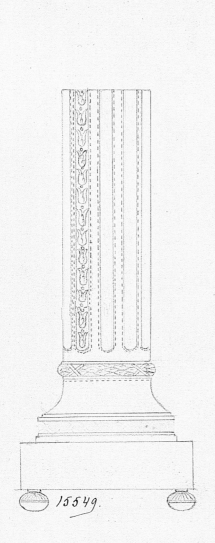

15549.

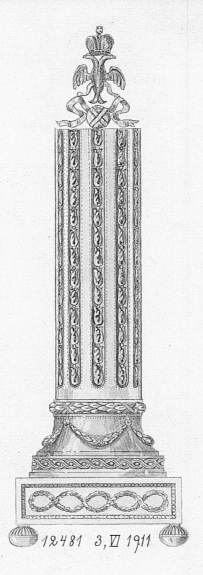

12481 3,VI 1911

12819.13.IX.1912.

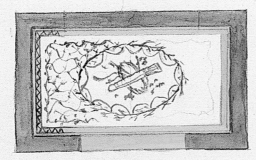

15176

Drawings of hardstone birds completed in Wigström's workshop in 1911, including a goose from Sandringham created for Queen Alexandra (Pl. 111).

1912. Her popularity reached new heights during the 1904-5 Russo-Japanese War, when she gave charity concerts for the wounded and financed her own corps of nurses to care for them.[52]

Foreign admirers of Fabergé

Fabergé first opened an office in London in 1903, with the aim of offering his most eminent customers, King Edward VII and his consort Queen Alexandra, the possibility of discussing commissions and viewing select collections in private. The patronage of the British Royal family was to prove invaluable to Fabergé, for it brought in its wake the elite of Edwardian society. For the exiled Russian Grand Dukes, Fabergé's showrooms became something of a place of pilgrimage, for here was an authentic piece of their yearned-for "Mother Russia". Very soon the clients of the London branch included members of the aristocracy and wealthy bourgeoisie from all over the European continent, and the showrooms became a meeting place for this international clientele. To provide far-flung clients with their full service, Fabergé's representatives made regular trips to Paris, Rome and Cannes, where many of their habitués resided.

King Edward VII and Queen Alexandra had become fascinated with the work of Fabergé through the influence of the Queen's sister, Empress Maria Feodorovna, whose gifts today form the core of the important Fabergé collection in the possession of Queen Elizabeth II. The King and Queen were regular visitors to the Fabergé premises, as were their son, the Prince of Wales and future King George V, and his consort Princess Mary, the Princess Royal and future Queen Mary. King Edward commissioned and bought for the Queen innumerable objects, most of

Queen Alexandra was very fond of animal hardstone figurines such as this agate owl. Her husband King Edward VII commissioned from Fabergé models in miniature of all her favorite animals at Sandringham.

Queen Alexandra of Great-Britain (right) and her sister Dowager Empress Maria Feodorovna were both avid collectors of Fabergé's creations.

The Prince of Wales, later
King Edward VIII
and subsequently Duke
of Windsor, wearing
the robes of the Order of the
Garter in 1911, on the
occasion of his investiture.

them hardstone animals. The most important occasion for a Fabergé gift each year was the Queen's birthday on 1st December.[53]

Perhaps the most significant event in the creation of Queen Alexandra's collection was King Edward's decision in 1907 to commission miniature sculptures of the animals at Sandringham, from the favorite royal dogs and the Derby-winner Persimmon, to the full gamut of domestic and farmyard animals: dogs, cats, cocks, turkeys, geese, shire horses and heifers. Sculptors came from St. Petersburg to model the pets and other animals in wax before they were carved in hardstone.[54] One inhabitant of the royal farmyard, a goose carved in quartzite, is illustrated in the Wigström album (Pl. 111 - opposite).

One of King George's commissions is a cameo portrait on a miniature easel of his son Edward (Pl. 319 - below), dressed in the mantle he wore at his investiture as Prince of Wales in 1911.

The Wigström album includes drawings for many of the London clientele's commissions.[55] Those for Leopold de Rothschild include a cigarette case and holder, a minaudière, pill box , table clock, and large frame with his racing colors in gold and blue stripes (Pl. 103, 141, 161, 197, 207, 311 and 327). A pair of cigarette boxes in lilac enamel (Pl. 215) was purchased by Baron Konrad G. Meyendorff, attaché at the Russian Embassy in London, just in time to celebrate the tenth anniversary of his marriage to Nadine Luginin. A cigarette case in gold, decorated with opaque stripes of white enamel and bearing the crowned monogram "A" (Pl. 400 - see p.151) was a gift by Prince Alexander of Battenberg to his cousin, Victoria Eugenia, Queen Victoria's granddaughter and the future Queen of Spain.

In 1911, King George V commissioned from Fabergé's London branch a miniature easel to hold a portrait of his son the Prince of Wales, a drawing of which appears on plate 319.

PLATE 169

Drawings of gold, enameled and jeweled belt buckles and cloak clasps.

A silver gilt table box in red enamel (Pl. 211 - see p.108) was purchased by a brewer named Mr. R. [for Robert] Younger, whose name occurs frequently among the clients at Fabergé's London branch.

A *minaudière* in pink *guilloché* enamel (Pl. 197 - see p.84) has three compartments, the top one for a powder puff, the middle one for lipstick and the lower one for coins. An engraved inscription inside, reading "Trouville 1911" in Cyrillic script, reveals that this lovely gift was offered after a visit to the fashionable French resort. It was sold by the London branch to a gentleman by the name of I. Groult.[56]

An unusual circular pill box in gold, with an enameled top and a Renaissance-style motif (Pl. 215 - see p.115), was completed at the workshop late in 1913. Made for the London branch, it remained in stock until December 1916, when it was purchased by the American millionairess Mrs. William Bateman Leeds. Fabergé's best client at the London branch during its two last years, Mrs. Leeds spent £2,766 in 1915 alone, and while shopping for Christmas in 1916 bought 26 items for £1,130.

Princess Cécile Murat[57] was the most fascinating among Fabergé's French customers, one of the grand ladies of her time and a central figure in *haute société*. Among her innumerable purchases from Fabergé, as well as from the renowned Parisian jewelers, the most intriguing was a series of over twenty cigarette cases, commissioned for delivery each year a few days

The grey enamel box shown on plate 13 of the album is now in the Cincinnati Art Museum. It features a cameo representing supplicants before Alexander the Great.

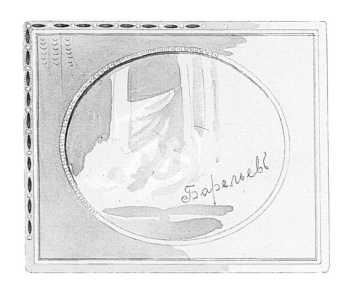

12415 3/VI 1911

12415 3/VI 1911

12520 25/VI 1911

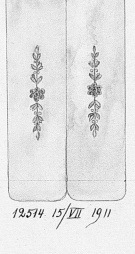

12514 15/VII 1911

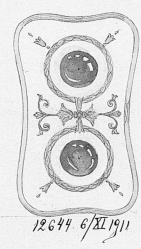

12644 6/XI 1911

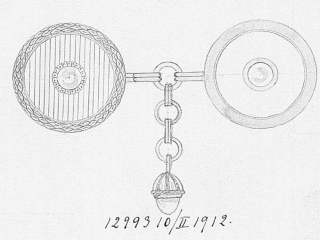

12993 10/II 1912.

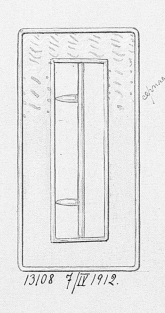

13108 7/IV 1912.

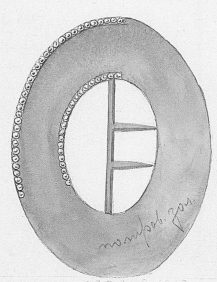

13355. 20.9.1912.

№ 13383
11 ОКТ 1912

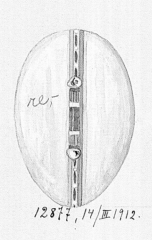

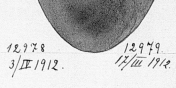
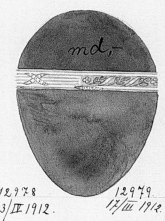

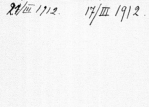

12877, 14/III 1912.

12980   12981
22/III 1912.   17/III 1912.

12978   12979.
3/IV 1912.   17/III 1912.

12991 17/III 1912

12992. 14/III 1912.

13050 13/III 1912

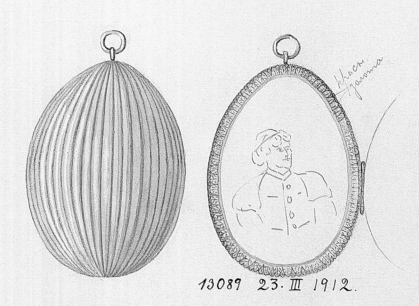

13089   23. III 1912.

The 1912 Imperial Easter egg was a gift from Emperor Nicholas II to his mother, shown here with her daughter Grand Duchess Xenia Alexandrovna.

before New Year's. All were gifts to the same close friend of the Princess, M. Charles Luzarche d'Azay. Agathon Karlovich Fabergé, Carl Fabergé's second son and close collaborator, described the singular approach adopted by the Princess: "The French Princess, Cécile Murat, who was related to Emperor Napoleon I, was one of our most interesting customers. This fabulously wealthy and well-traveled lady was not popular among the Parisian jewelers as she was most irrational and contrary when it came to her annual commissions for a gold cigarette case for her husband [sic]. Her only argument was that each case she commissioned should be of the finest possible workmanship, the best which human hands could possibly create. 'I want the case to be a souvenir from my trip', the Princess would say on her return from China or Africa, and as a rule chose the most complicated design, so one can well imagine the animosity towards her felt by our Parisian colleagues. We, however, gave in to the perils of making these cases and our craftsmen always saved our honor. We usually worked on the Princess's cigarette case for a whole year. Their price therefore rose to several million Finnish marks calculated in today's money. But the price was never discussed. It was the quality that counted."[58]

Thanks to information supplied by a friend of M. Charles Luzarche d'Azay, the delightful story of this most unusual and enduring friendship can now be revealed.[59] It apparently began during the first years of the 1900s and was to last

The "Napoleonic" Imperial Easter egg of 1912 commemorated the Russian victory over the French armies in 1812. It is now in the New Orleans Museum of Art, on loan from the Matilda Geddings Gray Foundation.

A nephrite egg bonbonnière similar to the example shown on plate 189.

PLATE 189

Drawings of the "Napoleonic" Imperial Easter egg of 1912, in gold and green enamel on a *guilloché* ground, and of nephrite and enamel bonbonnières in the form of eggs.

A caricature of
Charles Luzarche d'Azay,
the French gentleman to
whom Princess Cécile Murat
presented over twenty
Fabergé cigarette cases as
New Year's gifts.

to the day of the Princess's death in 1960. Whenever Princess Murat made one of her regular visits to the spa town of Evian, Luzarche d'Azay would go too, arriving at the hotel a few days later. Dinner in the hotel was always taken at separate tables. When in Paris, Luzarche d'Azay dined on Saturdays at Rue de Monceau, where the Princess had her *hôtel particulier*. Luzarche d'Azay lived near by, and they were often to be seen promenading together. His friend describes him thus:

"He was a very nice and pleasant man with a great sense of humor, witty and funny. He was well-bred and distinguished, although he did not have a particular interest in literature (not even a library of his own), nor was he interested in music. Not a dandy, but still an elegant man, he lived in the 'old style', and always dined in black tie, even when he was dining alone at home. He was not a wealthy man, but had a financial background which made it possible for him to live as a *rentier*.

In his youth he had enlisted as a simple soldier and became very interested in the 'military style of life', although he retired from the army after the Great War. Therefore, he never gained a higher military rank than *maréchal des logis*. 'Le tout Paris' said that Mr. Luzarche d'Azay was part of the Secret Service after the War, but there is no evidence of this."

Once, during a discussion with Charles Luzarche d'Azay, his friend brought out an elegant Fabergé cigarette case from his pocket, mentioning by whom it was made. To this Luzarche d'Azay replied that he himself had about twenty cases by Fabergé, and that they were given to him by a lady. When Luzarche d'Azay died in 1961, leaving no heirs, he bequeathed all his belongings to museums. The twenty cigarette cases are now in the collection of the Musée des Arts Décoratifs in Paris, and three are depicted in the Wigström album

A gold *minaudière* in pink *guilloché* enamel, completed in St. Petersburg on 13 April 1912 and collected in London by I. Groult as early as 27 April 1912.

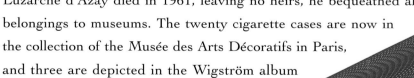

(Pl. 141 - see p.65, 217 - opposite, and 400 - see p.151). A few cases are inscribed with an enigmatic inscription in Arabic and in several of them the Princess's profile portrait is concealed in a hidden compartment.

It may seem to the reader that this chapter has dealt with matters which have little apparent significance for the goldsmith's art. But, at every period in history, the jeweler's art reflects the society in which he worked. Not only do these creations mirror the tastes and preferences of individuals within that society, but they also encapsulate much of its lifestyle in general. Objects of precious metal, often commissioned as tokens of love or appreciation or as mementoes of important events, are intended to outlive their donors and original owners. For posterity, an object with a provenance becomes a piece of living history. Thus it is that, through the pages of the Wigström album, with all their many references to so many well-known patrons, we are able to relive the lost world of imperial St. Petersburg.

A gold cigarette case, shown on plate 217, presented to Charles Luzarche d'Azay in 1914.

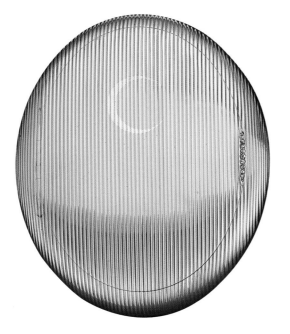
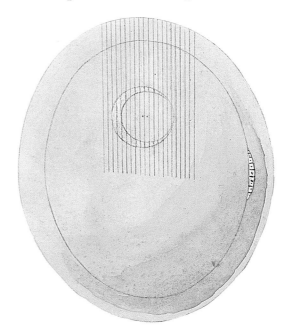

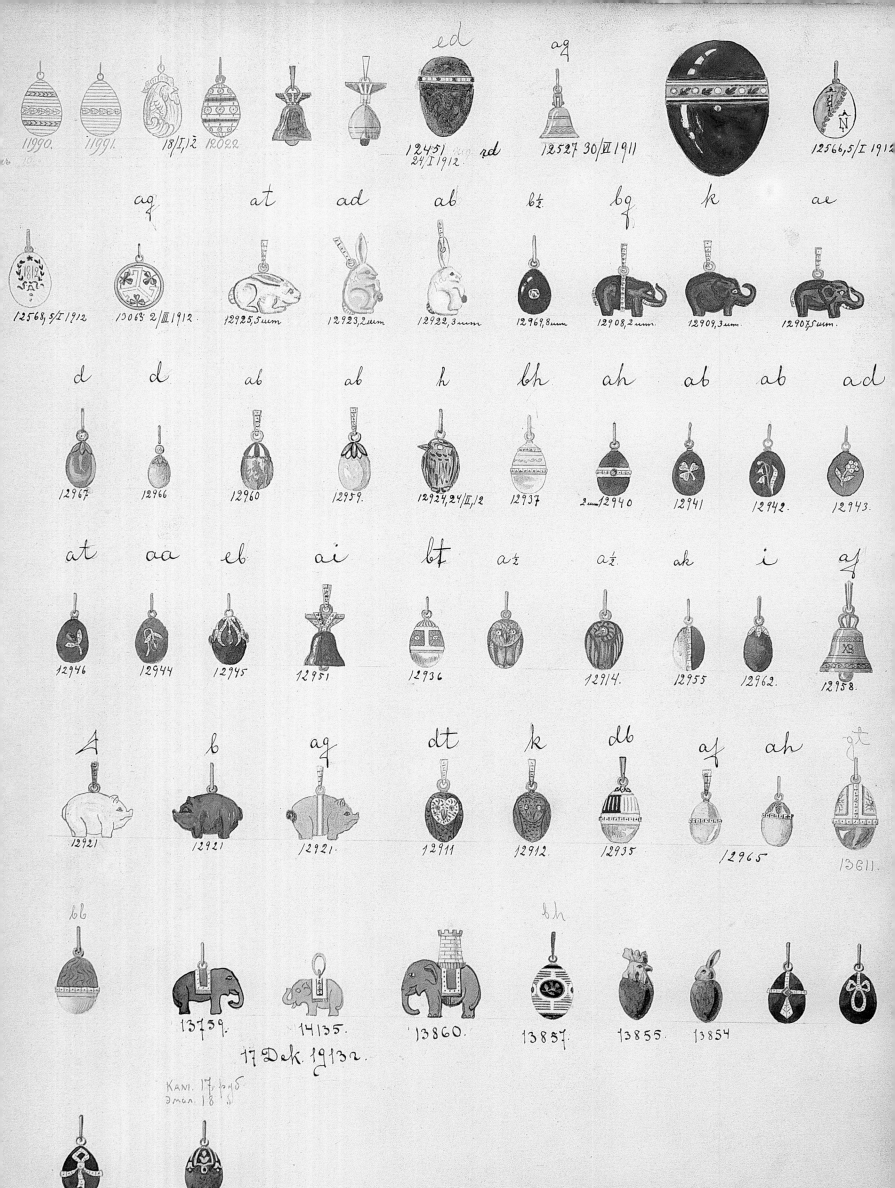

11990. 11991. 18/I.12 12022.

ed

12451
24/I.1912 rd

ag

12527 30/VI.1911

12566,5/I.1912

ag

12568,5/I.1912

at

13063 2/III.1912.

ad

12925,5 шт.

ab

12923,2 шт.

b½

12922,3 шт.

bg

12969,8 шт.

k

12908,2 шт.

ae

12909,3 шт.

12907,5 шт.

d

12967

d

12966

ab

12960

ab

12959.

h

12924,24/II.12

bh

12937

ah

2 шт. 12940

ab

12941

ab

12942.

ad

12943.

at

12946

aa

12944

eb

12945

ai

12951

bt

12936

a½

a½.

12914.

ak

12955

i

12962.

af

12958.

A

12921

b

12921

ag

12921.

dt

12911

k

12912.

db

12935

af

ah

12965

gt

13611.

bb

13759.

14135.

13860.

bh

13857.

13855 13854

17 Dek. 1913г.

Kam. 17 руб.
Эмал. 18 б.

Chapter Three

Fabergé
and the Royal House of Thailand

Toward the end of the nineteenth century, the Emperor of Russia and the King of Siam embarked on a relationship that would flourish for decades through both family contact and an extravagant exchange of gifts. In 1890, Tsarevich Nikolai Alexandrovich, son of Emperor Alexander III, later to become Nicholas II, made a week-long stop in Siam (known today as Thailand) during a naval cruise. As a "token" of gratitude for the visit, King Chulalongkorn (known in spititual lineage as Rama V) presented the Tsarevich with two elephants and a white monkey. Later, the Emperor would bestow on the King the order of St. Andrew, the highest order of the Russian Empire: in return, the King granted the Emperor the Order of Chakri, the highest Siamese order.

His Majesty King Chulalongkorn, who had been crowned in 1865 at the age of fifteen, guided his nation through the perilous era of great European expansion. Recognizing the futility of overt resistance to Western military might, he launched instead a series of internal reforms with the aim of modernizing his nation to standards of European culture. This mission took him in 1897 to Russia, then a major European power. One significant result of that trip was the first official diplomatic exchange between the two countries. Another was the strong personal ties forged with Emperor Nicholas II.

A variety of Easter egg pendants, one of which, in white *guilloché* enamel (middle), is in the Royal Collection, Thailand, the two others featured on plate 191.

After his trip to Russia in 1897, King Chulalongkorn of Siam forged strong personal ties with Emperor Nicholas II. Here they are seen together at Peterhof, the summer residence of the Imperial family.

Prince Chakrabongse in Russia

The visit proved so congenial, in fact, that the King had one of his sons, the fifteen year-old Prince Chakrabongse, remain in Russia to study. Prince Chakrabongse's extended stay proved highly formative in the strong

PLATE 191

Drawings of miniature Easter eggs and other pendants in hardstone, gold and enamel.

An elephant carved in nephrite, with a gold and enamel howdah.

Carl Fabergé traveled to Siam in 1908, providing the court with a number of exquisite creations such as this frame containing a miniature of King Chulalongkorn.

relationship between the two nations. The Prince was treated by the Imperial family as one of their own, attending the Corps des Pages and eventually joining the Hussars, where he rose to the rank of Captain. In 1908 he was granted permission to wear the full-dress uniform of the Life Guards of the Hussar Regiment in the rank of Lieutenant.

In 1906 Prince Chakrabongse married a Russian lady, Katerina Desnitskaia, the daughter of a Serving State Councilor, former head of the Judicial Court in Volynsk. The wedding was performed in a Greek Orthodox Church in Constantinople. Katerina, who was given the title Duchess of Pispoulok (an outlying district of Bangkok) bore Prince Chakrabongse a son, Prince Chula Chakrabongse.

Born in Siam, he became a writer and published the story of his parents in a book, *Born at Parusakavan*. He married an Englishwoman, Elisabeth Hunter, with whom he had a daughter, who still lives in England. Upon his birth, Prince Chula Chakrabongse received a small cup by the House of Fabergé from the wife of the Russian ambassador to the Siamese court.

During Prince Chakrabongse's years in Russia, Siam became the first non-European Royal House to collect and commission objects from Fabergé.

There were commemorations, such as photographs of King Chulalongkorn's 1897 visit taken at the Imperial summer palaces, some at Tsarsköe Selo and others at Peterhof (see previous page), framed in exquisite Fabergé frames of silver gilt and *guilloché* enamel; gifts from Emperor Nicholas II made especially by Fabergé

Another similar frame held in the Royal Collection, Thailand, containing a photograph of King Chulalongkorn.

While in St. Petersburg, Prince Chakrabongse was welcomed by the Imperial family as one of their own and took part in every aspect of court life. He is shown here wearing a seventeenth-century Russian uniform on the occasion of the 1903 Winter Palace costume ball.

Overleaf:

PLATE 195

Drawings of various boxes (compacts, *minaudières*, nécessaires) in gold and enamel.

PLATE 197

Drawings of *minaudières* in gold and enamel.

for the Siamese Royal family; gifts commissioned by the Prince; and objects ordered by other members of the Siamese monarchy who clearly recognized Fabergé's unique magnificence.

Carl Fabergé in Siam

In 1904, King Chulalongkorn invited Carl Gustavovich Fabergé to visit Siam. Four years later, despite the extreme difficulties in travel and the continual threat of epidemics of diseases such as smallpox, cholera, and even plague, Fabergé undertook the trip, booking an entire train car to carry the nephrite candelabras, sacral vessels, and other large objects bound for Bangkok.

There the King awarded him the title of Court Jeweler and Enameler. As the first and only firm to conduct business with the Siamese Royal family and aristocracy, he was granted commissions for jewelry, *objets de fantaisie*, and religious objects.

Fabergé subsequently traveled to India as well, where he was taken on a tour of the maharajas' palaces, deriving both inspiration and an expanded knowledge of oriental forms as well as gaining new clients.

Miniature Buddhist relics containers known as *chedi* were among Fabergé's royal Siamese commissions. In Buddhist nations such as Siam, monumental *chedi* contain sacred relics of Buddha. One such sacred miniature designed by Fabergé is only 6.5 centimeters in height. Carved out of solid nephrite, it is superimposed with a square 14-carat gold structure studded with rose diamonds. Above this rises a ringed red jade cone with a single pearl finial.

In 1910, not long before his death, King Chulalongkorn gave a dinner in Bangkok in honor of the newly appointed Russian ambassador, Anton

Fabergé, appointed "Court Jeweler and Enameler" to the King of Siam, created this nephrite Buddha, originally in the Royal Collection.

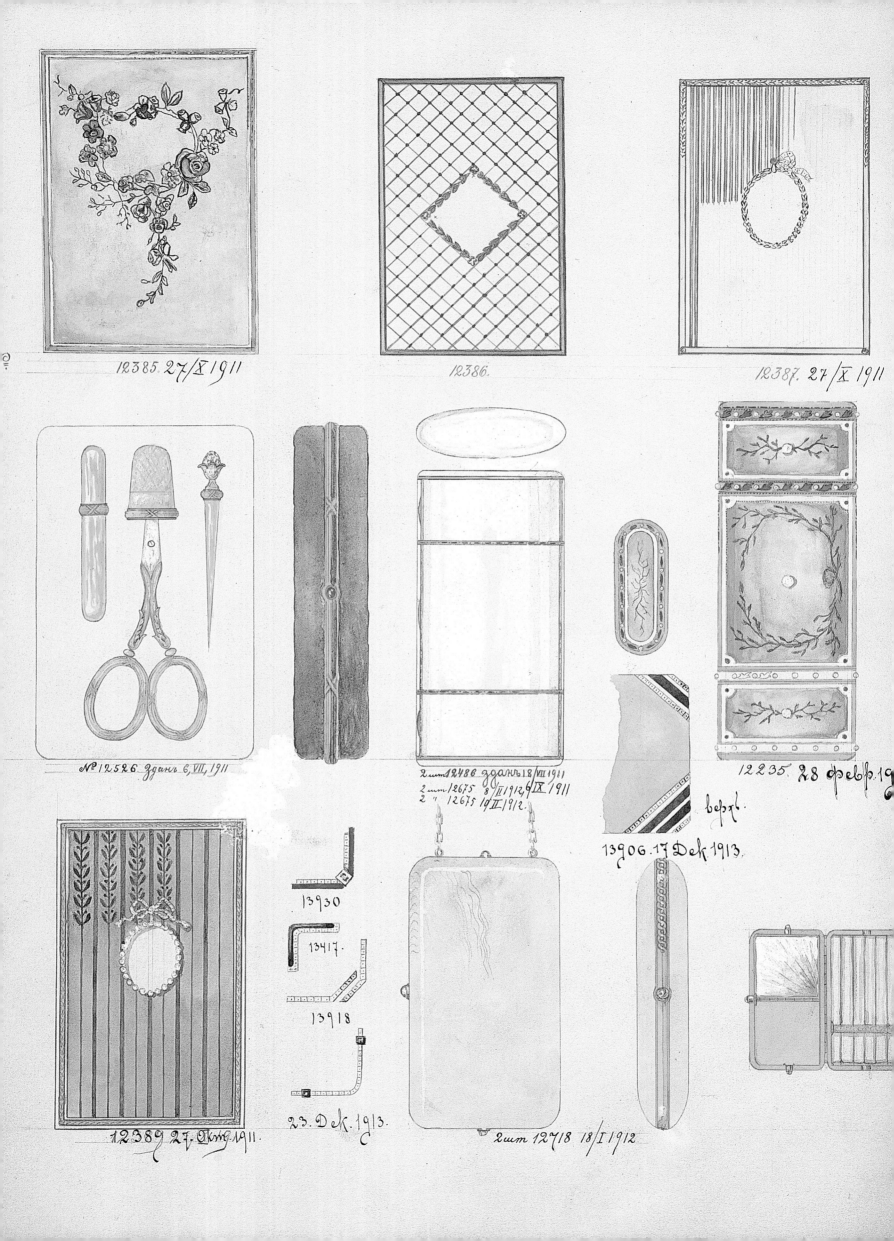

12385. 27/X 1911

12386.

12387. 27/X 1911

№ 12526. 3дань 6. VII. 1911

2шт. 12486 3дань 18/VII 1911
2шт. 12675 8/II 1912 6/IX 1911
2 " 12675 19/II 1912.

12235. 28 февр. 19

13906. 17 Дек 1913.

верхъ.

12389 27. Окт. 1911.

13930

13417.

13918

23. Дек. 1913.
С

2шт 12718 18/I 1912

ПУХОВКА

ГУБНАЯ ПОМАДА

МОНЕТЪ

13041. 13. IV. 1912.

12707 14/III 1912.

13412. 26. VI. 1913.

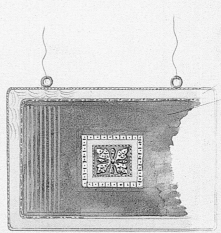

12243. 18. VIII. 1912.

опалъ
син. опа

13602. 27. VI. 1913.

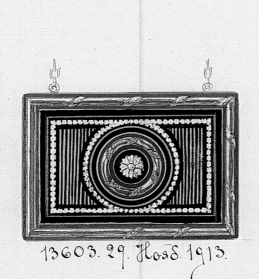

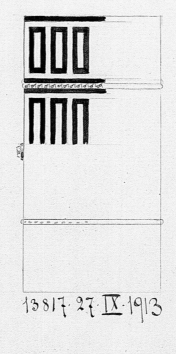

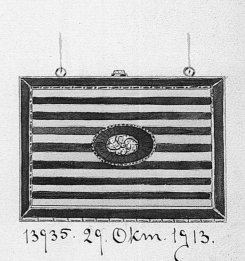

13603. 29. Нояб. 1913.

13817. 27. IX. 1913

13935. 29. Окт. 1913.

PLATE 201

Drawings of various
nephrite boxes with jeweled
and enameled mounts.

Another Fabergé jewel in
the Royal Collection,
Thailand, is this diamond-set
pendant containing
a miniature portrait of King
Mongkut, King
Chulalongkorn's father.

Planson-Rostkov. In a letter to Nicholas II, Planson described the King in full regalia, "without any medals, except for the Russian ribbon and badges of the order of Andrei Pervozvannyi." Equally impressive, the Queen wore across her shoulder the ribbon of St. Catherine the Martyr and on her chest a diamond badge given to her by Empress Alexandra Feodorovna in memory of the Holy Coronation. All these majestic decorations were made by Fabergé. (The badges, along with brooches and crowns, were created in a lot of eighteen pieces that was presented to the Queen and all the Siamese princes in 1896). Planson also described in his letter the exceptional warmth of Crown Prince Maha Vajiravudh who recalled meeting the ambassador in Peterhof in 1897. "He had changed very little", Planson wrote, "the same calm, majestic bearing, which lent a certain charm to his slight and handsome build."

Maha Vajiravudh was publicly crowned Rama VI in 1911 (a private coronation had taken place the year before). Despite the great distance, considerable expense, and threat of disease, emissaries from Britain, Sweden, Denmark, the Austro-Hungarian Empire, France, Spain, Japan, Norway, Germany, Italy, Belgium, the Netherlands, and the United States traveled to Bangkok for the celebrations. Emperor Nicholas II sent his personal representative Grand Duke Boris Vladimirovich.

The presence of so many figures from royal European houses was due to the diplomatic talents of Prince Chakrabongse, who had toured and been received in almost all the European courts. These royal receptions, particularly the 1910 coronation of King George V in London, had exposed Prince Chakrabongse to European ceremonial grandeur.

As a result, he was able to ensure that his brother's coronation expressed a comparable splendor. Even the accommodations for foreign dignitaries

A nephrite box with an
enameled gold mount,
from the Royal Collection,
Thailand.

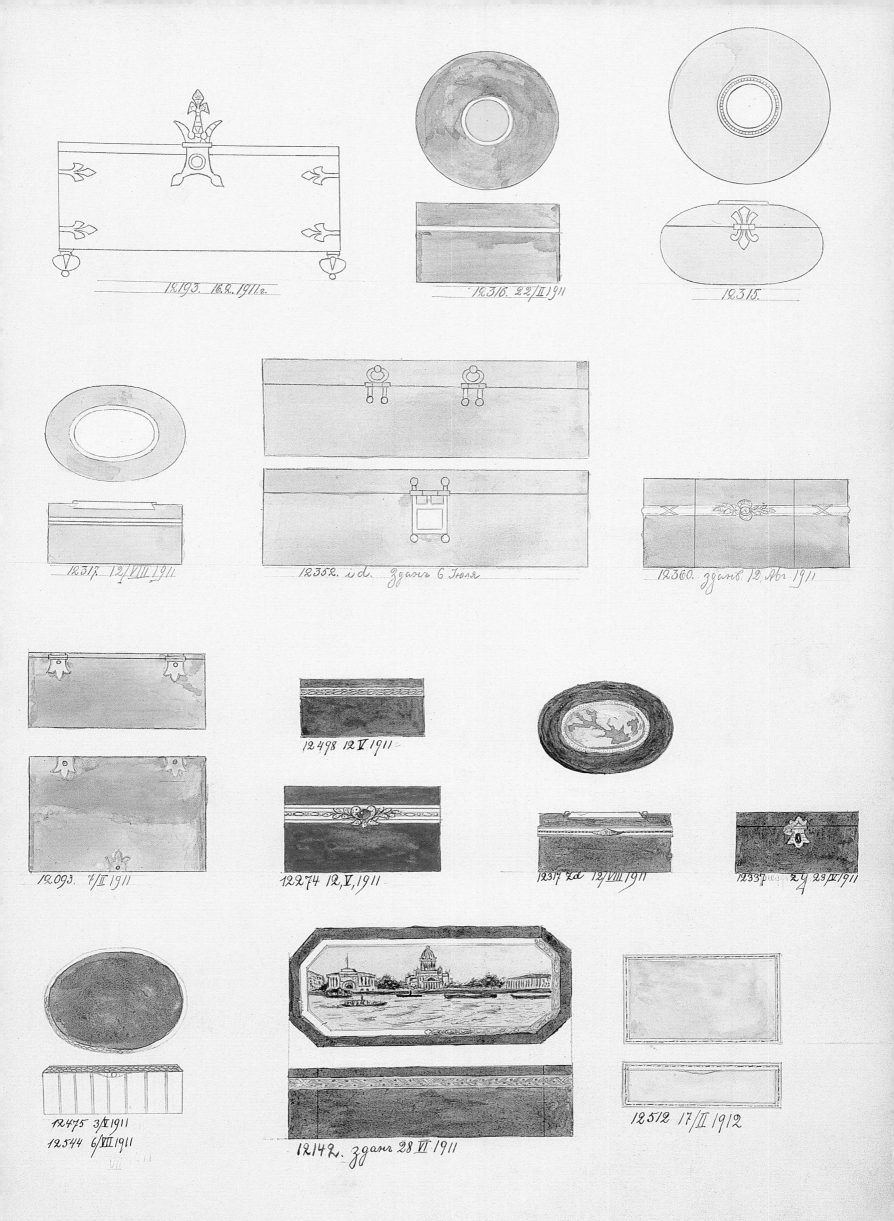

12193. 16.2.1911.г.

12316. 22/II 1911

12315.

12317. 12/VIII 1911

12352. i.d. Здань 6 Гюля

12360. Здань 12 Авг 1911

12093. 7/II 1911

12498 12 V 1911

12274 12.V.1911

12317 Zd 12/VIII 1911

12337 перед. 24 23/IV 1911

12475 3/V 1911
12544 6/VII 1911

12142. Здань 28 VI 1911

12512 17/II 1912

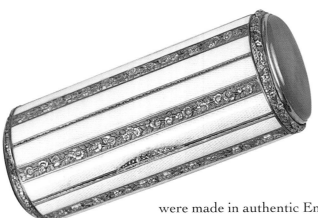

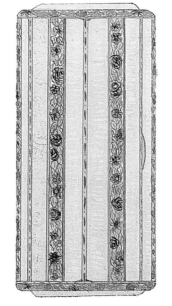

The Royal Collection, Thailand, includes a cigarette case (Pl. 127) with two oval-shaped pink agate lids revealing a cigarette holder on one side and a match compartment on the other.

A cigarette holder in amber, gold and white *guilloché* enamel, delivered to the Royal Collection, Thailand, together with the cigarette case shown opposite.

were made in authentic English comfort: quartered in the court palaces and state residences, they were chauffeured in magnificent automobiles and carriages by liveried drivers and coachmen.

Rama VI's public coronation combined ancient Buddhist rituals, costumes, and ceremonies with European-style opulence. Representatives of the Royal court, the diplomatic corps, and a select circle of Siamese officials and soldiers gathered to witness the King's ascent to a special throne, carved in stone. After placing upon his own head a gold and diamond crown, he was regaled with a symphony of trumpets, drums, and conch shells and proceeded to a balcony where, from a gilded throne, he received the adulation and shouts of joy of his people.

Celebratory events continued for hours, nights, and days, including all manner of banquets, theatrical performances, bazaars, and receptions. The King made several royal processions through the streets of Bangkok. All ages and classes of the country's populations turned out to cheer him. The processions were followed by a ceremonial swim in the Menarne River, which was crowded with sumptuously decorated boats rowed by oarsmen dressed in Siamese costumes resembling Russian finery. The culminating event was a spectacular military review of thirty thousand soldiers that lasted until three o'clock in the morning.

Fabergé's commissions from King Rama VI

After his coronation, the new king pressed Fabergé into action. He commissioned, among other notable objects, a large chalice for the memorial temple of his father, made of green Siberian nephrite and decorated with gold, pink enamel, and diamonds. He also ordered two large nephrite candelabra for electric lights, made in the style of Louis XVI.

Wat Arun, the Temple of Dawn in Bangkok, featured on the lid of a carved nephrite box in the Royal Collection, Thailand (below, and Pl. 219, p.111).

Another of the great Fabergé works believed to have been commissioned by Rama VI is a sacral water bowl twenty-five centimeters in diameter. It is carved from a single piece of nephrite into the shape of a Buddhist monk's alms bowl and supported by molded gold figures of the three Hindu gods, Brama, Vishnu, and Shiva. The deities are represented in the form of Mythical animals: Brama, the creator of the world, as a wild gander; Vishnu, the protector and savior of the world, as half-bird, half-man; and Shiva, the creator, sustainer, and destroyer, as a bull. Each highly detailed figure is elaborately decorated with rubies, diamonds, and emeralds. Arranged in a triangle to carry the alms bowl, the figures stand on a similarly configured nephrite base, which, in turn, stands on three reeded silver-gilt bun feet.

The sacral water bowl was used by the King and held holy water for administering the Oath of Allegiance to high court officials, a ceremony held in the Temple of the Emerald Buddha. The gold from which the three deities were formed is said to have been supplied by the King himself. The piece is signed by Henrik Wigström.

In Russia, Buddhists considered Siam to be the source of Buddhism, and they acknowledged the King of Siam as the head of their religion. Between 1913 and 1915, the largest Buddhist temple in Europe was built in St. Petersburg, despite the Russian fear of Japanese influence. Rama VI presented a gilded copper sculpture of the Buddha Shakvamuna as a gift to the temple. Planson, the Russian ambassador, sent a bronze Buddha. He, like other foreign emissaries, collected Siamese sculpture during his tenure. These works had great scholarly and artistic value, and their focus was Buddhist sculpture.

The sepia enamel miniature of the Temple of Dawn on a *guilloché* ground demonstrates the high degree of craftsmanship attained in the Fabergé workshops.

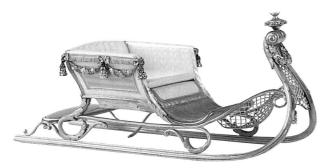

A miniature sledge in translucent *guilloché* enamel (Pl. 205, see p.98), the seat opening to reveal a compartment; from the Royal Collection, Thailand.

Among the numerous Fabergé items commissioned by Rama VI was a large Buddha carved from a single piece of nephrite. A masterpiece of serenity, the sacred figure, created in 1914, was presumably intended for the Prince's personal worship, and was kept in the King's private chapel in the Grand Palace. Thirty-seven and a half centimeters in height, it sits on a lotus base with its posture — legs folded, the soles of its feet turned upwards — and its meditative gaze expressing the Buddha's state of enlightenment.

Another Buddha, this one a miniature only nine centimeters in height, is believed to have been commissioned by Prince Chakrabongse as a gift for his brother Prince Mahidol, and was kept in the Royal family's chapel in the Chitralada Palace. Also carved from a solid piece of nephrite, it sits on an 18-carat gold base decorated with a multicolored enameled pattern of lotus petals. Its hands rest one on top of the other, with palms upward in the posture of meditation. A gold aureole with red enamel "flames" representing the emanation of divine light from the crown chakra, rises from the tiny figure's head. Two others by Wigström are known, but with nephrite "flames" (see below and p.89).

Fabergé and the Royal Collection of Thailand

The Fabergé pieces in the collection of the Royal House of Thailand may be divided into two groups. One consists of those pieces, like the sacral water bowl, while considered to be the King's personal property, must be passed on to his successor. The second group includes pieces that are the personal property of the King, and which may be disposed of as he sees fit. The large nephrite Buddha made for Rama VI in 1914 may well have been one of the last *chefs-d'œuvre* to come out of the House of Fabergé, which closed in 1917. The First World War, the Russian Revolution, the Imperial

A nephrite Buddha on a gold and enamel base, originally a Royal Siamese commission.

A nephrite cup with
an elaborate jeweled and
enameled gold mount,
from the Royal Collection,
Thailand; shown on plate 251.

family's assassination and the end of Rama VI's reign, in 1925, brought to a close the relationship between the Imperial House of Russia and the Royal House of the nation to be known as Thailand.

During the Second World War, the Fabergé objects were sent out of the capital for safekeeping. Although they were later returned to the Grand Palace in Bangkok, they remained packed away for decades.

In 1981, Her Majesty Queen Sirikit of Thailand visited Hillwood in Washington D.C., the former home of Marjorie Merriweather Post, now a public museum. Mrs. Post had amassed a superior collection of Russian imperial art during her marriage to the American ambassador to Russia and Her Majesty wished to view the Fabergé objects on display. On the day of her visit, she wore an exquisite brooch by Fabergé containing the likeness of a member of the Royal family.

A year later, the Fabergé collection of the Royal House of Thailand was at last unpacked for the occasion of the Rattanakosin Bicentennial. In 1983, a small group of researchers from Hillwood was granted the opportunity to travel to Bangkok and view the collection. Many of the pieces were still in their original boxes.

In 2000, A La Vieille Russie, the celebrated New York antiques and jewelry shop, featured Fabergé pieces from the Royal Collection, Thailand, in an exhibition of works by Henrik Wigström, Fabergé's chief workmaster and goldsmith. The exhibition was developed, in part, to assist the *Thai Support Foundation*, which helps to preserve native crafts and assist Thai farmers and craftsmen, under the patronage of Her Majesty Queen Sirikit. The exhibition, which also traveled to the New Orleans Museum of Art, marked the first time any of the Fabergé pieces from the collection of the Royal House of Thailand had ever left that country.

Nephrite elephant pendants
with diamond-set loops and
mounts, shown on plate 191.

12310 орл ра — 25/IX 1911

12359 нефр d у — 12/VIII 1911

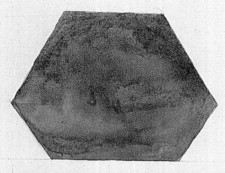

12360 нефр г d здань 12/VIII 1911

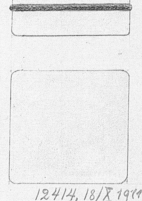

12414, 18/X 1911

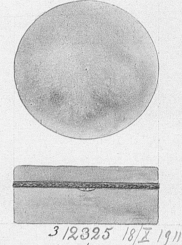

3 12325 18/X 1911.
2 9/II 1912.

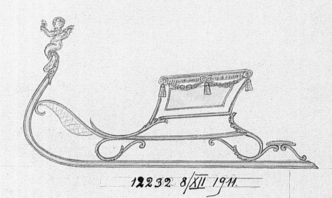

12232 8/XII 1911

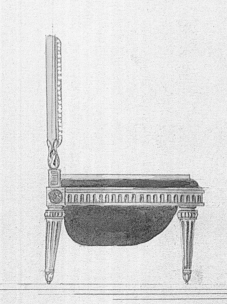

12417   Сдан 26го Мая 1915.

Chapter Four

The Triumph of Style
An Analysis of the Master's Designs

A gold-mounted and enameled rhodonite box, completed in Wigström's workshop in 1911 (see opposite), today in the FORBES Magazine Collection, New York.

A perusal of the many pages of Wigström's album reveals a multitude of beautifully rendered designs in watercolor for items that were made by his workshop. On leafing through this album, one cannot help but be struck by the Louis XVI style that dominates the drawings. The pieces drawn and painted here remain true to an era characterized by form, proportion, and color. Plate after plate seems to stand as a tribute to classical discipline. The principles of balance and proportion dominate these drawings for cigarette cases and parasol handles enriched with minimal decoration in the form of laurel borders and diamond-set crossed ribbons.

Classicism revisited

The leading jewelers who had won renown in the nineteenth century prospered yet further in this period known as the Belle Epoque. Jewels became emblematic of an age of wealth, social glitter and creative innovation. It was an era of tremendous novelty, characterized by major scientific breakthroughs such as the domestic use of electricity, the invention of the motorcar and the camera, and major medical findings. It was also a period of widespread peace. For the leisured classes it was a time of an opulent lifestyle graced by sensuality, femininity and sophistication. Jewelry was worn with passion and pride both in Paris and St. Petersburg, and women were exquisitely turned out in the most lavish and elegant costumes. It was quite normal for a lady to change her attire several times during the course of a day, according to her various social engagements, such as lunch followed by tea, and afterwards the ballet and supper. As Consuelo Vanderbilt, the American heiress who visited St. Petersburg in 1902, observed: "Russian women had a parure of jewels to match each dress."[1]

A salt chair in gold, nephrite, enamel and pearls (Pl. 205), from the collection of the Cleveland Museum of Art.

PLATE 205

Drawings of boxes in hardstone and enamel, including a sledge and Louis XVI-style salt chair.

A gold-mounted nephrite presentation box, the lid set with a portrait miniature of Emperor Alexander II in an oval frame of diamonds and rubies.

The social scene was a stage on which the wealthy might parade their status and it was against this setting that the great jewelry and fashion houses now enjoyed the patronage of emperors and grand dukes, emirs and princes, tycoons and businessmen, *demi-mondaines* and actresses, singers and ballerinas. Competition between jewelers and rivalry amongst their clientele was intense, resulting in the creation of a steady stream of fabulous jewels.

The St. Petersburg establishment naturally wished to uphold the existing political and social structure. Fabergé and other leading jewelers responded to this desire by continuing to create jewels in a vein that was synonymous with the established order and therefore attractive to their rich and aristocratic clientele. After all, the House of Fabergé was a business, and it was Carl Fabergé's flair for recognizing the nature of his clientele's tastes that ensured its survival. In short, his decision to remain within the classical canon was in part a logical response to the political and social arena of his time. Fabergé's London branch especially epitomized this complex relationship between client and purveyor, evolving into a private viewing room and meeting ground for the King and Queen and their entourage, as well as for the magnates of the epoch.

From Paris to St. Petersburg, wealthy society continued to emulate the lifestyle of the eighteenth century, as exemplified by the elegance and splendor of Versailles. Accordingly, its members favored architects able to design their mansions along classical lines. Styles of interior decoration followed in the same taste, as did fashions in dress, to complement the whole. Jewelry, which defined social status, was therefore required to conform to the same look. Fabergé, along with Cartier and other leading firms, was quick to respond to an increasing demand for objects and jewelry conceived and executed in this restrained and elegant manner. The fashion in jewelry

Countess de Hohenfelzen later Princess Paley, the wife of Grand Duke Pavel Alexandrovich, youngest son of Alexander III.

A gold and enamel oblong snuffbox with chamfered corners, the lid with a diamond-set flower basket, a common motif in Wigström's work.

Drawing of a cigarette
case in gold, enamel
and diamonds, from plate 137.
The design reveals the strong
influence of the Louis XVI-
style in Fabergé's work.

known as the "garland style", featuring ribbon bows, and neo-classical laurel and acanthus swags, was adopted by leading firms, reaching its culmination in the 1890s and lingering on until the eve of the First World War. Similarly, the ordered, symmetrical, and repetitive patterns of eighteenth-century architecture, wrought iron and metalwork designs were adapted by the craftsmen for gold and silver objects.

The gem-set mounts of a series of traditional mesh evening bags, for example, feature such ornaments in various permutations (Pl. 81-89). A "romantic" version of this style is illustrated by the bonbonnière with a diamond ribbon interlaced with enameled roses against a matte enamel lilac ground (Pl. 159 - see p.73). Laurel leaves and swags lend themselves to adorning columns (Pl. 165), as well as the tapering handles of lorgnettes and fans (Pl. 25, 41 and 45). The miniature holder (Pl. 165 - see p.76), and the nephrite gold-mounted clock (Pl. 299 - see p.131), both in the form of columns, suggest the elegance and wealth of their owners. The fans on plate 25 (see p.18), meanwhile, conjure up visions of the flirtatious unfolding of their panoramas with the deft flick of a jeweled wrist. Such is the power of the images evoked by this exquisitely contrived craftsmanship and the skilful juxtaposition of motifs, colors, and materials. It is this remarkable combination that ensures the continuing magic of Fabergé to this day. The revival of the techniques of the eighteenth-century French goldsmith's art (*guilloché* enamel) provided another logical pretext for Fabergé to create work reminiscent of the court of Versailles, with its many enameled bibelots, snuffboxes and fans. Various pieces from the reigns of Elizabeth Petrovna and Catherine the Great, in the Hermitage collections, furthermore served him as models for items that by their nature proved perfect vehicles for the display of his exquisite enamel work.

Matilda Kshesinskaia,
Prima ballerina
of the Mariinsky Theater,
photographed wearing
jewelry in the garland style.

A platinum-mounted
nephrite cigarette case,
the lid set with a diamond
heart enclosing
the Roman numeral XX.

PLATE 207

Drawings of small boxes
and bonbonnières in gold,
nephrite and enamel.

Miniature gold-mounted
enamel bonbonnière
in the form of an armchair
in the Empire style (Pl. 207),
the seat sliding to reveal
a compartment;
from the FORBES Magazine
Collection, New York.

A base of either gold or silver was first engraved with a geometric pattern
(*guilloché*), and this remained visible through the transparent enamel, which
was applied in five or six layers, each fired at a temperature of 700-850
degrees Centigrade. The resulting effect was similar to that of silk moiré,
with shimmering undulations heightened by light and shadow.

The astonishing palette of colors used by Fabergé for his enamels — num-
bering over 140 different hues — was unsurpassed by any other contemporary goldsmith.

At the time of the 1900 Paris Exposition Universelle, Fabergé's neo-classi-
cism attracted a number of caustic criticisms, mainly from the French press,
which contrasted it unfavorably with the popular loose and fanciful style of
art nouveau, or the "modern style", as embodied by Lalique and Fouquet.
Yet even his critics praised the quality of Fabergé's workmanship and his
unparalleled repertoire of enamel work, which earned him both the Grand
Prix and the Légion d'Honneur.

In view of the fact that emerging styles such as art nouveau flourished in
all the major European capitals during the first decade of the twentieth
century, it seems particularly puzzling that these vegetal and floral influences failed to take root in Wigström's idiom as expressed in this album.
Birbaum, Fabergé's head designer, observed that the "modern style", tanta-
mount to "dissoluteness of shapes and unrestrained fantasy bordering on
the absurd, could not attract designers who had become accustomed to a
certain artistic discipline.

We [Fabergé] naturally acknowledged the artistic value of objects created by certain individuals, such as Lalique, but we never tried to imitate
him: we thought it useless and we were right, for his imitators, while
unable to produce anything comparable to his masterpieces, lost their

A blue *guilloché* enamel
stamp box, similar to
the model in pink shown
on plate 207.

Drawing of a pentagonal
nephrite box from plate 203,
and a similar box
with a diamond and ruby
thumbpiece.

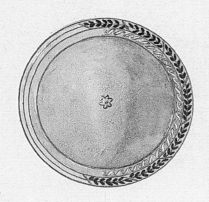

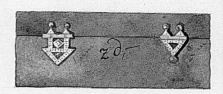

12876 24/II 1912.

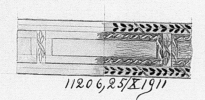

11206, 25/X 1911

12734 29/XI 1911

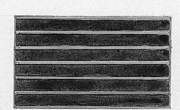

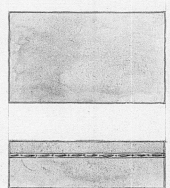

12679 24/XI 1911

12677 17/II 1912

12676 2 Шт 21/II 1912.

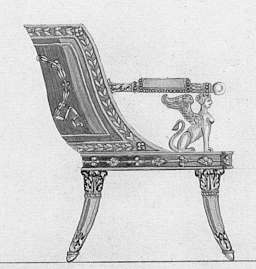

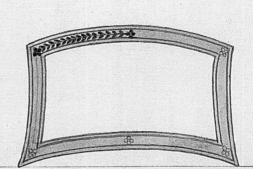

own originality."[2] In recognition of Lalique's talent, it was at Birbaums's recommendation that one of Fabergé's stone carvers, Derbyshev, was sent to Paris for several years to train under him.[3]

The craftsmen of Wigström's workshop continued to cultivate the style that best suited them. The Napoleonic Egg for 1912 (Pl. 189) — the only

Imperial egg commission documented in the album — is emblematic of the Empire style, with its arrangement of rosettes, acanthus motifs, and laurel wreaths, and illustrates this predilection perfectly. Although it commemorates the Russian victory over Napoleon, the egg is ironically in the French Empire style.

The choice of the classical style is significant, given the time at which the Napoleonic Egg was conceived. For beneath feelings of confidence in the social order and wealth of Europe and Russia there lay an undercurrent of foreboding and anxiety for the future, and for the challenges it might hold for the established order. This sense of instability was to be translated into a wealth of dynamic and revolutionary works in every field of the arts.

In Russia, Primitivist and Cubist artists such as Goncharova, Malevich, Tatlin and Rodchenko were breaking with the past, producing manifestos

Classical elements such as the repeating motifs of wrought-iron railings or bridges (here the Lion Bridge over the Ekaterinsky Canal in St. Petersburg) are often to be seen in Fabergé's designs.

This drawing from plate 313, and the actual corresponding table clock in rhodonite with silver-gilt mounts, demonstrate the restrained use of decorative motifs to create a sober and elegant design.

Drawing of a hardstone hand seal from plate 69, identical to the seal shown opposite.

A hand seal in lapis lazuli, gold, enamel and rose diamonds.

and exhibitions in which they protested against materialism and voiced their desire to build a new life with a new world view. In London, a major Post-Impressionist art exhibition featuring key works by Cézanne, Van Gogh, Picasso and Matisse was reviewed as the "Artquake of 1910".[4] Yet Wigström's album reveals no sign of these tumultuous undercurrents. The bounds of classicism are transgressed only on the rare occasions when he turns to historicism or the Orient for inspiration, or chooses a simplicity of style that foreshadows modernism.

Imprint of a Nation

The mid-nineteenth century witnessed the development of the Old Russian style accompanied by a general pursuit of Slav heritage, as may be seen in the art and literature of the time. Many artists turned away from the West and sought to create a new national culture, based on the Russian peasant vernacular and on long-neglected indigenous artistic traditions. Moscow became the focus for this national movement.

Most significantly, in 1850 the Moscow Art Academy made a momentous break with the St. Petersburg academic tradition of teaching, adopting a more liberal syllabus.

In the decorative arts, the tradition of Russian enamel work stretched back to medieval Kiev and reached its apogee in the Moscow Armory (*Oruzheynaya Palata*) in the seventeenth century. Surfaces were profusely decorated with stylized flowers, exotic birds, and scenes from folklore.

Moscow had always attracted the best goldsmiths and silversmiths, until the establishment of the new capital of St. Petersburg entailed the closing of the Armory workshops in 1727. As a result, the years that followed

The Russian style that was revived in the nineteenth century and up to the First World War influenced architecture (here the Isidore Yurievsky Church in St. Petersburg, built in 1907-8) as well as the decorative and fine arts.

12678 24/XII 1911

12430 15/II 1912

12608 23/XI 1911 3 шт

12754 1/XII 1911

12875 15/II 1912.

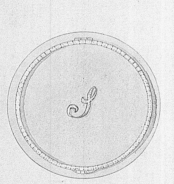

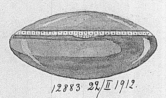

12883 27/II 1912.

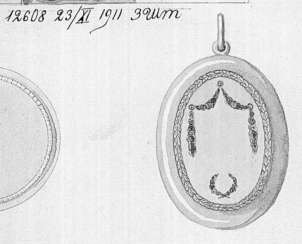

13046, 6/III 1912.

12988 17/III 1912.

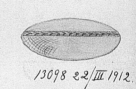

13098 22/III 1912.

№ 13283
18 ОКТ 1912

13143 18.V.1912.

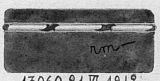

13060. 21. VI. 1912.

-12878. 18. VII. 1912.

№ 13283

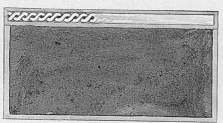

13312. 23. VIII. 1912.

12879, 23. VIII. 1912

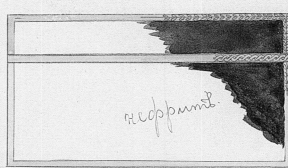

нефритъ.

13105. 5. IX. 1912.

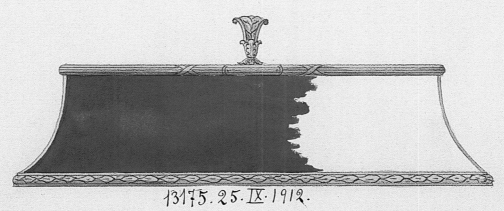

13175. 25. IX. 1912.

13232. 25. IX. 1912.

Previous pages:

PLATE 209

Drawings of pill boxes, bonbonnières, lockets and a table box.

PLATE 211

Drawings of a red enamel table box and four nephrite boxes.

A gold-mounted nephrite box similar to that drawn at the bottom of plate 209.

saw a decline in the traditional Russian style of enamel work and metal-work, with an emphasis on more Western themes. The traditional art was revived in the nineteenth century, however, when goldsmiths returned to their medieval heritage, rediscovering old techniques and reinterpreting them in their own language.

Years before the art nouveau movement became established, Fabergé and his Russian contemporaries were including renderings of floral and vegetal themes in their work, most notably in the form of sinuous vines and flowers encircling mythological birds which found their source in the Byzantine tradition and in the Solvychegodsk[5] enamels. The adherents of the so-called Old Russian style revived this folk craft in their houses in and around Moscow. In the 1890s, Princess Maria Tenisheva transformed her estate at Talashkino into a center for the study of vernacular styles, where traditional woodcarvings and textiles were collected and studied as sources of inspiration for contemporary art. Another such cultural commune was set up at Ambramtsevo, in the country estate of the Mamontov family, who were wealthy art collectors. Here, leading painters such as Vrubel, Vasnetsov, and Polenov lived and worked, similarly creating some of the most influential masterpieces of the time, based on old Russian motifs.

A silver-gilt and red enamel table box, drawn on plate 211 (previous page). It was sold through Fabergé's London branch on 14 October 1912 to Robert Younger for £60.

Madame Dmitri
Vonliarliarsky dressed as
the wife of a Russian boyar,
on the occasion of the
famous costume ball held
at the Winter Palace in 1903.

Independent silversmiths, notably Feodor Rückert who worked for Fabergé in Moscow, created enameled articles in the same vein.

Very much admired at the World Fairs, this work was described thus by a Russian contemporary: "There are some branches of industry where we, the Russians, can find no equals in Europe. These are the branches created by us personally, grown and developed in the Russian soil and bearing the imprint of the country. It is impossible for foreigners to imitate them."[6]

Traditionally, the Moscow clientele was not aristocratic but consisted rather of Old Believers, members of the intelligentsia, and merchants: sections of society who nurtured a deep sense of pride in their city and its former glory, coupled with a strong Orthodox faith. The type of objects that were made for the Moscow market tended therefore to cater to this taste. Furthermore, Moscow's strong economy allowed artists and craftsmen to depend less on the court and more on private sponsorship and trade. Moscow tastes were diametrically opposed to those of Fabergé's St. Petersburg clientele, who, as has already been seen, preferred Western styles, perceived as emblematic of progress and aristocratic chic.

The deep cultural differences between the two major centers were further magnified by the geography of Russia. The vast expanse of territory that separated the two cities was partly responsible for the rift that opened up between them. Communication problems furthermore served only to encourage the differences that already existed, and to foster a sense of cultural isolation. As a consequence, each city proudly cultivated its own distinct personality and heritage, as mirrored in the works of its native artists. To mark the tercentenary of the Romanov dynasty, the Moscow workshops

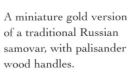

A miniature gold version
of a traditional Russian
samovar, with palisander
wood handles.

Fabergé's interest in other countries and earlier eras is illustrated by this Chinese nephrite cricket cage adapted by Wigström as a powder compact (Pl. 219).

PLATE 219

Drawings of bonbonnières and compacts, including an exquisitely carved nephrite box resting on miniature gold elephants and featuring on its cover *Wat Arun* (the Temple of Dawn) in sepia enamel.

created massive presentation bowls, caskets and *kovshi*[7] in the traditional Russian manner. With the exception of a Romanov breast badge made specifically for the occasion but completed in January 1914, (Pl. 79 - see p.46), the Wigström album, by contrast, contains very little to mark this momentous event.

The four Imperial Easter eggs for the years 1912 and 1913 are stylistically interesting. One, designed by Alma Pihl at the Holmström workshop, is very different from the other three in that its motif is derived from nature: a carved rock crystal egg containing a bouquet of white anemones, symbolizing the awakening of spring.

The Napoleonic Egg, illustrated in the album and discussed above, the Tsarevich Egg and the Romanov Tercentenary Egg all evoke great events from Russian history. They are embellished with symbols of the Russian Empire, such as the double-headed Imperial eagle, the Imperial coat of arms, the medieval Monomakh crown[8], or portraits of the Russian sovereigns. All this notwithstanding, the three of them are designed in the French taste.

From Antiquity to the Orient

Although the neo-classical style dominates Henrik Wigström's album, its plates are also dotted with articles inspired by Greek or Roman archaeological finds, as well as by Gothic, Renaissance and Asian artifacts. Beakers, bowls and boxes are reminiscent of Roman and Greek household wares, while a snuffbox and a series of jeweled crosses conjure up images of the Renaissance.

Other jewelers besides Fabergé, such as Cartier, Boucheron and Chaumet, were also actively engaged in seeking new sources of inspiration at this

The *Wat Arun* - Temple of Dawn table box depicts the temple built for King Rama II in Bangkok, *c.*1815 (see also p.95). It is thought to have been one of the coronation gifts presented to King Rama VI in 1911.

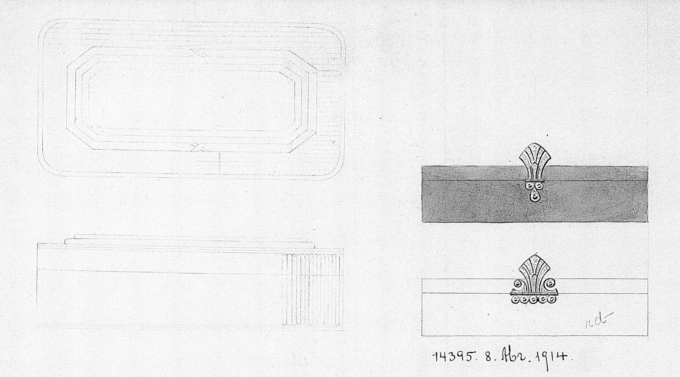

14395. 8. Abr. 1914.

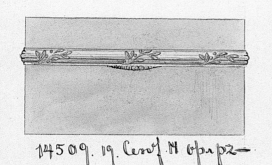

14509. 19. Cenf. 14 Opr.pz—

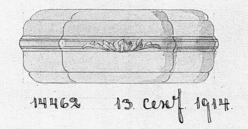

14462   13. Cenf 1914.

14467. 13. Cenf. 1914.

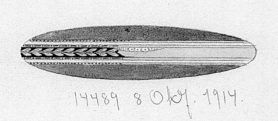

14489 8 Okr. 1914.

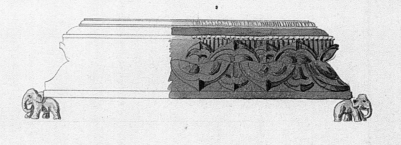

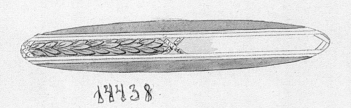

14438

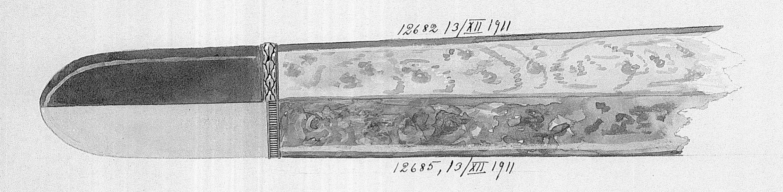

12682. 13/XII 1911

12685, 13/XII 1911

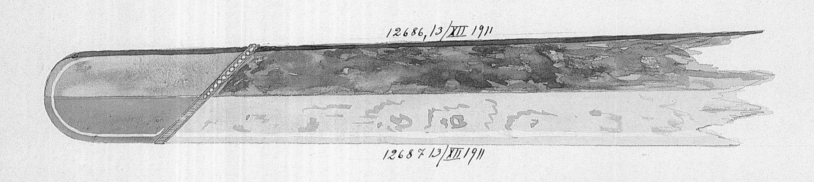

12686, 13/XII 1911

12687 13/XII 1911

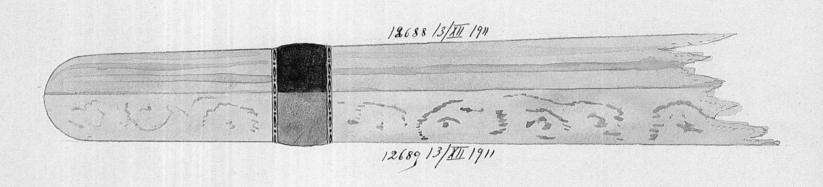

12688 13/XII 1911

12689 13/XII 1911

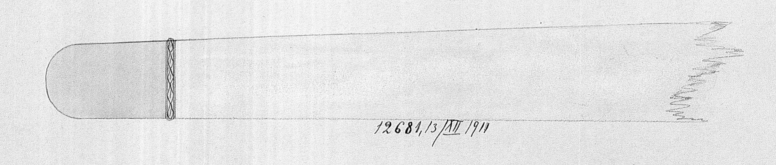

12681, 13/XII 1911

12680. 13/XII 1911

11875 *ly* /16/Ⅵ 1911

12444 *pe* 16/Ⅵ 1911

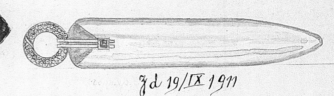

zd 19/ⅠX 1911

92 74 *m* 15/Ⅶ 1911

12442, 28/ⅩⅠ 1911

№ 1 3 2 7 5
26 СЕН 1912

12610, 28/ⅠX 1911

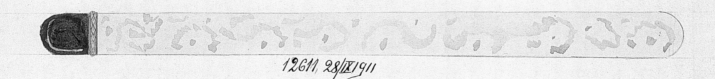

12611, 28/ⅠX 1911

лип pd, 12438, 28/ⅠX, 1911 *хрус i,—*

12584, *л ч,—*

Previous pages:

PLATE 231

Drawings of large paper-knives comprising blades of various woods — including birch — mounted in gold and enamel. They demonstrate Fabergé's flair for using even the simplest of indigenous materials in an elegant and decorative manner.

PLATE 233

Drawings for paper-knives in nephrite, gold and birch wood.

Drawing of a gold ring in the antique style, taken from plate 93.

time, whether from the Orient or from Russia. When Diaghilev's *Ballets Russes* took Paris by storm at the height of the Belle Epoque in 1909, for example, the show also proved a revelation to contemporary fashion designers and jewelers. The vibrant and revolutionary spectacle of the Russian dancers, draped in exotic costumes and moving to an unorthodox choreography against sets created by Leon Bakst, acted as a catalyst for artists in all fields. Subsequently, Charles Jacqueau, Cartier's chief designer, was taken by his mentor to Russia.[9] Couturiers such as Paul Poiret and Mariano Fortuny y Madraz, who not only dominated the Paris fashion scene but also worked as interior designers, creating items such as cushions, textiles, lamps and decorative panels, were also swept up in this surge of revolutionary creativity, producing colorful designs in exuberant materials. Fortuny observed in his notes: *"Que le dessin d'un tissu n'est pas la fantaisie d'un artiste, c'est l'objectivation d'un moment à travers l'artiste qui est le jouet inconscient du milieu, du temps dans lequel il vit..."*[10]

Fabergé's *ateliers*, by contrast, remained untouched by the magical costume and stage designs of the *Ballets Russes*, as demonstrated by the absence of drawings displaying their influence. The qualities that so entranced the European public, essentially alien and fairy-like as they were, perhaps seemed too close to home to Russian audiences, who failed to be similarly mesmerized. It was with this factor in mind, indeed, that the impresario Sergei Diaghilev conceived the ballet company for export rather than for home consumption.

Instead, Fabergé's designers turned to earlier ages for their models, one of the first examples being the Scythian period of the third and second centuries B.C. The firm won a gold medal for replicas of Kerch antiquities executed by the workmaster E. Kollin as early as 1882, at the Pan-Russian

A nephrite paperknife with reeded gold mount and diamond-set borders, also set with one large diamond and one cabochon ruby.

A carved nephrite oblong bowl with gold feet, similar to a drawing featured on plate 251. Sold by Fabergé's London branch, it bears English marks for 1912.

A gold-mounted oval lapis lazuli bowl in the antique manner and its corresponding drawing, taken from plate 257.

Art and Industrial Exhibition in Moscow. Fabergé continually delved into the past for historical models that might serve as inspiration for his designers. His formative years were spent within sight of the *Grünes Gewölbe* in Dresden, which housed the Treasury of the Saxon Electors, and as a young man he was greatly influenced by a lengthy tour of the jewelry centers of Europe. For some twenty years subsequently, he assisted the Keeper of the Imperial Hermitage in restoring, appraising and cleaning its precious objects — including the treasures displayed in the jewelry gallery. In the Hermitage Museum, Fabergé and his craftsmen had numerous opportunities to study ancient gold jewelry, mechanical clocks made by James Cox, figurines by Melchior Dinglinger, and an array of eighteenth-century snuffboxes. The album in turn includes a series of objects that reflect the antique as a source of inspiration, including a lapis lazuli bowl with Roman caryatid handles (Pl. 257 - above), three rings with snake and dolphin terminals (Pl. 91 and 93 - opposite), and numerous other items evoking daily life in Herculaneum and Pompeii.

Moving forward in time, the ornately enameled and jeweled openwork handle designs (Pl. 263 - see p.121, and Pl. 265 - see p.123) for a series of nephrite presentation trays are reminiscent of Renaissance work. Similar influences may be seen in the shell-shaped hardstone bowl resting on a pair of dolphins (Pl. 253 - overleaf), as well as the small circular snuffbox, elegantly enameled in a design of black arabesques around a central mask (Pl. 215 - right). It becomes clear from these works that Fabergé had passed on to Wigström his understanding and love of historical design. The series of pendants (Pl. 77 - see p.38), including a large cabochon amethyst flanked by nymphs and suspending pear-shaped pearls, and two smaller cross pendants, may be traced back directly to Renaissance models.

Drawing of a circular gold and black enamel bonbonnière in the Renaissance style, taken from plate 215.

Drawing of a lapis lazuli bowl in the Renaissance taste, taken from plate 261.

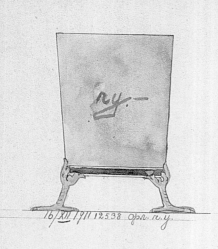

16/XII 1911 12538 орл. лу.

12549 нефр. ту. 15/VII 1911

12599 zd. - лу. 11.IX.1912.

12308 6/XI 1911

12471 11/VII 1911

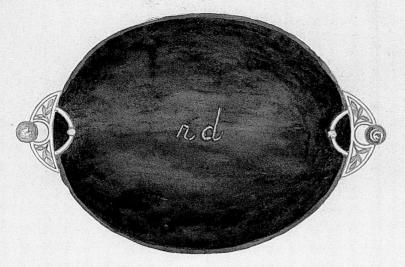

12441 16/XI 1911

12469 28/II 1912

12614 18/X 1911

12651 18/X 1911

12706 20/X 1911

12622, 14/XII 1911

Previous pages:

PLATE 253

Drawings of various oval
dishes, a bowl and a cup,
in gold-mounted hardstone
and purpurine.

PLATE 255

Drawings of various
dishes, predominantly
in nephrite, and an
openwork tea-glass holder.

PLATE 259

Drawings of various
dishes in hardstone,
including a gold-mounted
and enameled salver
with a moss agate panel.

Fabergé encouraged his master designers and craftsmen to seek out the most successful forms of artistic expression and skill, whether in eighteenth-century French enamel work or Saxon stone carving. In this process, the modern artist's integrity remained intact if his work also expressed his own creative ideas. Instead of yielding his originality to the strength of the sources from which he borrowed, he accepted these earlier aesthetic principles not as fixed codes, but rather as vital and pliable elements to be adapted to his own invention. This ability to borrow and adapt from different eras and civilizations informs the album. The eclectic quality of the design may be seen, for example, in a baroque-inspired medallion and cross (Pl. *77* - see p.38), a medieval-inspired pendant and brooch (Pl. *77* and *93*), and a Moorish-inspired cigarette case (Pl. *129* - see p.54).

Twice a year, a representative of the firm would travel to the East — to Siam, China, and India — to meet with important clients and take orders. As Peter Schaffer describes in his essay in the present volume, the King of Siam was one of Fabergé's important clients until the Great War. The album includes a number of objects made for him, predominantly in nephrite, reminiscent of the Orient's most prized stone, jade.

According to Birbaum, Carl Fabergé's younger brother and collaborator, Agathon, "sought inspiration in antique objects and in oriental styles that were little known in Russia at the time."[11] Although he was no longer living during Wigström's tenure, Agathon Fabergé's influence was still felt by the designers. It is possible, indeed, that his surviving designs and library were used as inspiration for the firm's work.

The drawings in the album are not always linked directly to a specific historical style, but are sometimes purely personal in conception. This is the case with the unusual rhodonite

A circular gold-mounted
snuffbox sold to Leopold de
Rothschild. The two
articulated Harlequins on the
lid and base dance the *cake
walk* when the box is shaken.

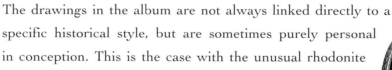

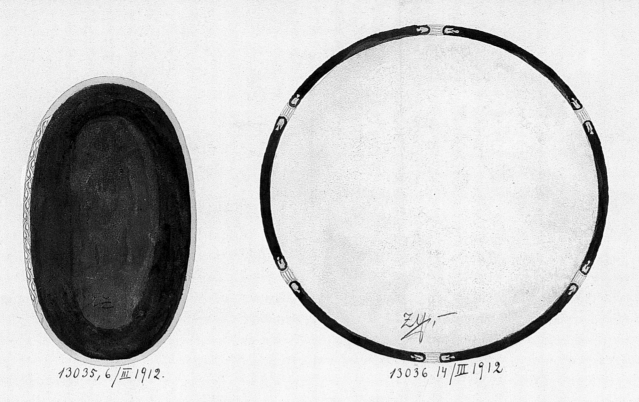

13035, 6/III 1912.

13036 14/III 1912

2 Stück

13626. 29 III 1913.

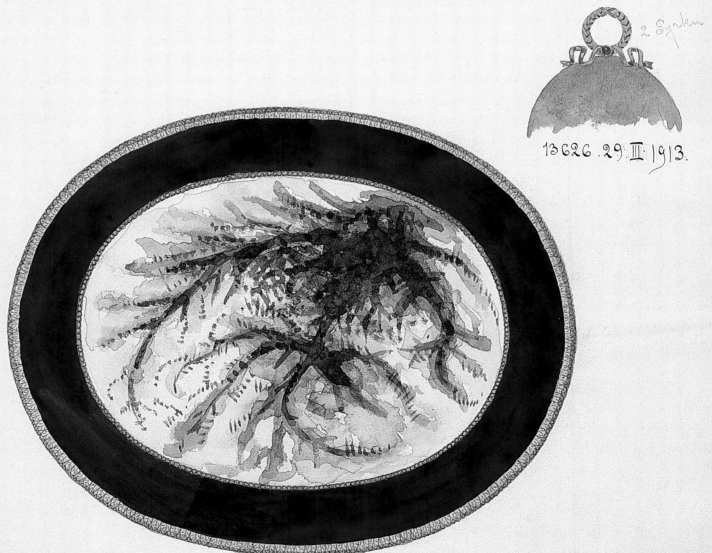

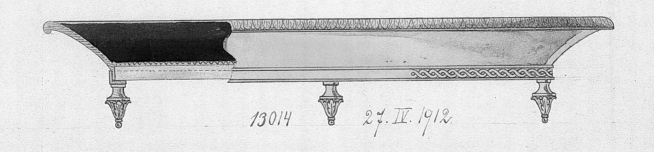

13014   27. IV. 1912.

mantel clock on plate 295 (see p.130), with two haunting black owls perched menacingly above the dial in a manner reminiscent of the writings of Edgar Allan Poe. It evokes something of the National Romanticism then so popular in Finland, the native country of many of Fabergé's workmasters and craftsmen. Was this clock a private commission or simply an unexpected whim on the part of the designer? Similarly surprising are a hardstone elephant with its howdah serving as a clock (Pl. 309 - see p.135), and the chalcedony bowl with a bathing beauty poised on either side (Pl. 265 - overleaf). The sedate nature of the album as a whole is relieved by the introduction of such unusual pieces, adding a note of humor and enchantment.

A miniature water bucket in nephrite with its bracket-handle enameled in translucent strawberry red. It is similar to that shown on plate 263.

Fascination with nature

Apart from the styles discussed above, jewelers turned to the natural world as a source of inspiration. Some, such as Lalique and Fouquet, were swept up into the art nouveau movement and became staunch critics of Cartier and Fabergé, whom they regarded as traditionalists.[12] Dismissing them as out of touch, they scorned their lack of interest in the new "vegetal" approach that had permeated contemporary architecture and fashion design. Supporters of art nouveau, and most especially the jeweler-goldsmiths of the time, found in its asymmetrical and irregular lines a certain vitality and freedom of expression.

An informal group photograph of Emperor Nicholas II and members of the Imperial family at Krasnoe Selo, in the summer palace of Grand Duke Vladimir Alexandrovich, *c*.1904.

Fabergé allowed himself freedom of another kind. Considering himself an artist-jeweler, he relied less on the intrinsic value of his materials than on their aesthetic quality. Although he was criticized for the lack of art nouveau influence in his work, Fabergé was

PLATE 263

Drawings of presentation *kovshi*, bowls and various objects, together with the gold and enamel nephrite presentation *kovsh* shown in the middle of the plate.

13735. VII. 1913.

13812. 29. X. 1913.

13947. 27. Янв. 1914.

13379 19. XII. 1912

14. февр. 1914

13966. 9. Янв. 1914

13606 22. XI. 1913.

A gold-mounted rectangular rhodonite box with emerald green *guilloché* enamel bands, an example of Fabergé's elegant use of Russian minerals.

PLATE 265

Drawings of various hardstone cups, including the nephrite cup in the antique style with cagework mount shown below, an unusual chalcedony bowl with two gold figurines, and a *kovsh* handle richly set with gems.

nonetheless directly inspired by nature. Throughout his career, his *œuvre* is punctuated with objects made of various types of wood and stone.

Russian artists and those from neighboring countries had worked intimately with wood for centuries. The great variety of species available was traditionally integrated into functional items such as the early peasant *kovsh*; later, under Fabergé's creative direction, these same woods, including most notably Karelian birch and palisander, were carved into cigarette cases and various other pieces.

Similarly, Russia had a long tradition of using its natural mineral wealth for the production of other useful items. As early as the first quarter of the eighteenth century, a major collection of minerals was cataloged at the Art Cabinet in St. Petersburg, founded by Peter the Great, and in the 1770s the leading goldsmith J.P. Ador is reported as having one "of the most beautiful natural science collections which contains many minerals from Siberia and other parts of Russia as well as beautiful precious gems."[15] The lapidary workshops that existed in Peterhof, Ekaterinburg, and Kolyvan were still active in the early twentieth century. The discovery of new minerals had a revitalizing effect on the industry, and encouraged a growing interest in experimentation with manmade substitutes.

In Wigström's work, the reinvention of purpurine, a simulation of red stone made from glass, is illustrated by an oval dish (Pl. 253 - see p.116), table clocks (Pl. 303 - see p.132) and a small Easter egg pendant suspended from a horseshoe (Pl. 187). Painted enamel was sometimes made to imitate moss agate, but most frequently gold or silver are used in straightforward combination with

A nephrite cup with a silver gilt mount enriched with rubies and sapphires, today in the Virginia Museum of Fine Arts, Bequest of Lillian Thomas Pratt.

12676. 9. Янв. 1914.

14256

14077.

14469. орл. ет—

PLATE 267

Drawings of *kovshi* and a
cup in the Roman style with
a gold cagework mount
in the form of olive branches.

semi-precious stones such as nephrite (known in Russian as *orletz*), bowenite, aventurine, rhodonite, lapis lazuli, and multicolored agate. According to
archival material, the hardstone pieces characteristic of Fabergé's work
started to appear in the 1890s, when, after repairing a bouquet of chrysan-
themums made in China, he was inspired to make his own flower studies

Drawing of an intricately
worked frost-flower
jewel featured on plate 73.

using various hardstones.[14] The workshops fashioned
wonderful sprays of hyacinths, poppies, roses, and
other blooms, placed in rock crystal vases that
appeared to be partly filled with water. The exquisite
gem-set bouquets in the Hermitage museum, made
by the eighteenth-century court goldsmith Jérémie
Pauzié, were certainly a source of inspiration, as well

Fabergé's creations were
also inspired by nature.
He interpreted hoarfrost
as a series of diamond-set
jewels.

as the hardstone flower carvings created in the Peterhof and Ekaterinburg
lapidary works. Fabergé's skill in stone carving is further demonstrated in
the hardstone figurine of Dowager Empress Maria Feodorovna's Cossack
bodyguard (Pl. 113 - see p.51) and in realistically carved fruits which dou-
bled as functional objects. A carved bowenite pear, for example, serves as a
gum pot, with its detachable stem mounted as a brush (Pl. 5 - see p.15), a
pansy with finely painted petals makes a brooch (Pl. 77 - see p.38), and a
tea-glass holder is formed by an iris and its intertwined
foliage (Pl. 255 - see p.117). Even the simplest icicle, or frost-
flower, might find its way on to the hinge of a nephrite
cigarette case (Pl. 127), or the central panel of a circular
brooch and pendant (Pl. 73 - right). A series of hardstone
birds (Pl. 111), meanwhile, shows Fabergé's passion for
ornithology. His detailed studies of nature are pushed to the
point of humor when he unexpectedly supports a refined

Drawing of a gold miniature
easel with a framed panel
of moss agate (Pl. 345).
When completed, the actual
piece (today in a private
collection) was attributed the
production number 13437.

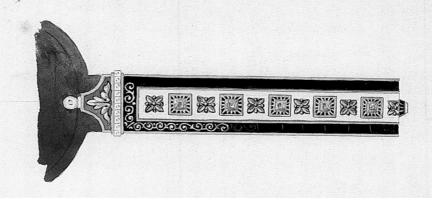

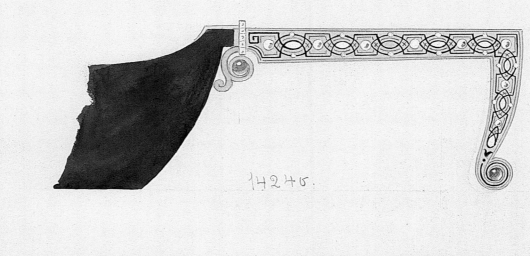

14245.

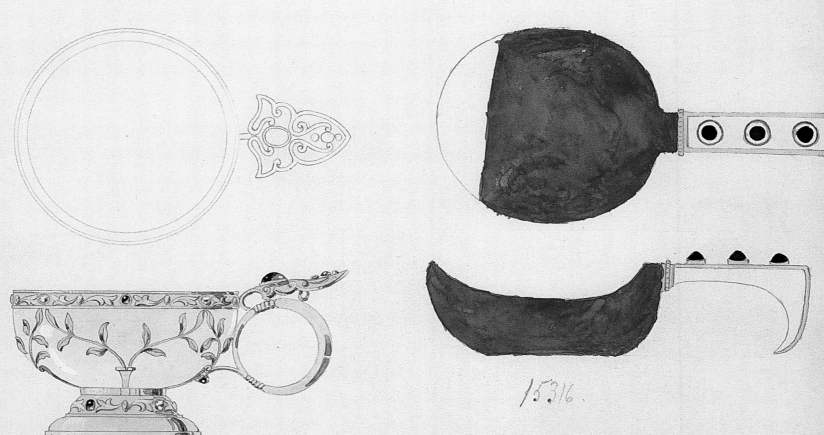

14559.

15316.

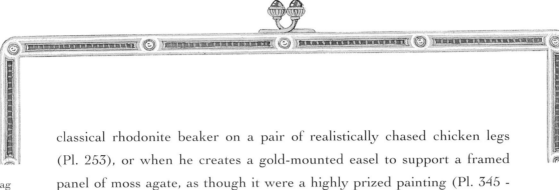

classical rhodonite beaker on a pair of realistically chased chicken legs (Pl. 253), or when he creates a gold-mounted easel to support a framed panel of moss agate, as though it were a highly prized painting (Pl. 345 - previous pages).

Drawing of an evening bag frame set with diamonds and square-cut rubies (Pl. 89)

Modernism

Fabergé is often criticized for working in a predominantly classical manner and for standing aloof from the maelstrom of contemporary artistic currents. In fact, however, his creativity and design skills were so advanced and so subtle that his work actually heralds some of the movements yet to come. While he assimilated styles of the past into his own vocabulary, he also designed pieces that were so streamlined that they might have been prototypes for art deco and modernist models of the industrial age.

The progression from the organized grammar and rhythms of classicism to the pared-down simplicity that defines modernism is a natural one. Both are disciplines: take for example the cigarette case, defined by its function and therefore limited to a rectangular or oval section. Given the tremendous popularity of this accoutrement for both sexes at the turn of the century, designers enjoyed considerable scope for playing with innumerable permutations of, say, vertical, horizontal, and diagonal stripes in varying widths. Classical swags and garlands thus eventually became stripped down and replaced by interlocking or varied vertical bands. The design no longer consisted of obvious decorative motifs, but rather became more integrated with the whole. The process was facilitated by the craftsmen's skill in the making of seamless hinges and concealed tinder-cord and vesta case compartments, which enabled the outlines of the case to be simplified as much as possible. The numerous cases featured in Wigström's album (for instance

Drawing of a lapis lazuli table clock with diamond-set bezel and outer frame (Pl. 301), together with a similar piece. They demonstrate Fabergé's ability to play with color and geometric forms in a manner heralding modern design.

Drawing of a gold and enamel hat pin in the Rothschild colors (Pl. 53).

PLATE 271

Drawings of enamel bell-pushes and bellpulls. Their basic forms of cylinder and cushion enabled the designer to play with the effect of foliated bands against various grounds.

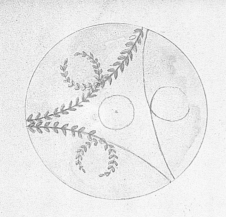

11478 16/VI 1911
Эмалевые 5/I 1912 10/II 1912. 5/III.1912.

2 шт. 18 ОКТ 1912

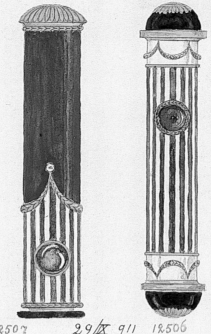

12507   29/IX 911   12506

12046   19/VIII 1911

12934 29.V.1912

12742. 28/II 1912.

6 Шт.

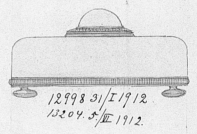

12998 31/I 1912.
13204. 5/III. 1912.

12746. 5/VI 1912

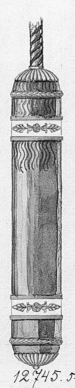

12745. 5.VI.1912.

12744. 5.VI.1912.

12743. 5.VI.1912.

5. Июня 1912.

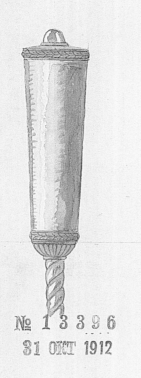

№ 13396
31 ОКТ 1912

№ 12763
15 НОЯ 1912

№ 13337
27 НОЯ 1912

14076. 21. февр. 1914.

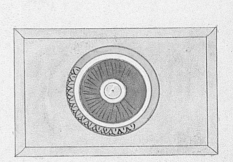

13607. 21. VI. 1913.

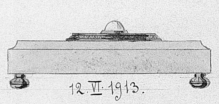

12. VI. 1913.

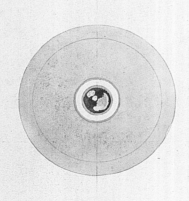

13537. 12. VI. 1913.

13861. 14. VIII. 1913.

13794. 14. VIII. 1913.

Дерево.

14154. 15. XI. 1913.

14152. 15. XI. 1913.

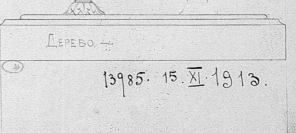

13985. 15. XI. 1913.

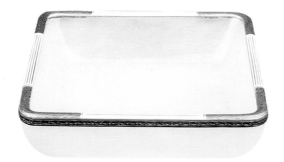

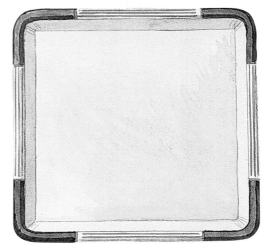

in plate 121 - see p.53) illustrate this development, while also demonstrating that when necessary a cigarette case might be designed in any style. This natural development towards a more simplified and absolute design, as exemplified by some of the Wigström pieces, was paralleled in the revolutionary architectural principles of modernist architects such as Mies Van der Rohe and Frank Lloyd Wright, both of whom were working at this time. Furthermore, Peter Behrens' design for the German Embassy, located a stone's throw away from Fabergé's showrooms in St. Petersburg, had been completed in 1911, with an interior already conceived in the art deco modernist vein. A preference for simple geometrical forms and for smooth, plain surfaces, for a monochrome palette, homogenous finishes, and avoidance of detail in relief, is apparent in the series of four circular match cases depicted on plate 101 (see p.44). A simple square dish with alternate reeded and dark borders, meanwhile, could have been made by Cartier at the height of the art deco period (Pl. 261 - above).

Also included in the album is a design that appears to be ahead of its time by several decades: a locket-pendant with an ingenious mechanism in the form of an accordion that allows ten photograph frames to be tightly packed within a globular shape less than five centimeters in diameter (Pl. 75 - see p.59). A hat pin (Pl. 53 - previous pages) designed in a spiral shape reminiscent of a futurist space center is another example of these "modernist" pieces which seem out of context in the album, and could easily date from a later period. Had Fabergé's work not been interrupted by the Great War and the Revolution, the glimpses of modernism already apparent in the album would most certainly have moved to the forefront of his *œuvre*.

Drawing of a gold table clock with opaque white enamel stripes (Pl. 301), and the corresponding object.

Drawing of a modernist bowenite ashtray taken from plate 261; a design so elegantly simple that it was later to be taken up by Cartier. The actual object (above) is now in the FORBES Magazine Collection, New York.

Overleaf:
PLATES 295 AND 299

Drawings of table clocks in hardstone and enamel.

PLATE 273

Drawings of hardstone and enamel bellpushes completed in Wigström's workshop from 1912 to 1914.

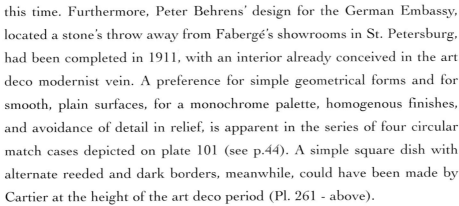

A bellpush in blue *guilloché* enamel, similar to the pink example shown on plate 273.

15001. Сдано 26го февр. 1916г.

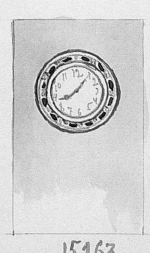

15023

15160

15163

14024.

12477 пирпр. vd 28/II 1912

12455 dy - 5/I 1912

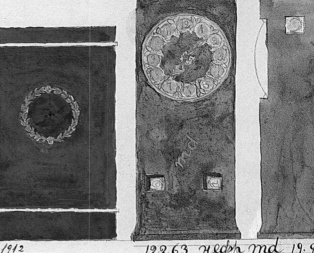

12263 нефр md 19.9.191

12423 25/X 1911

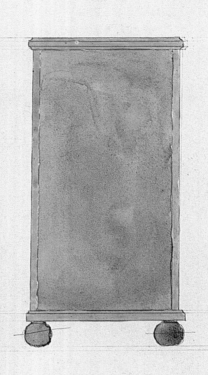

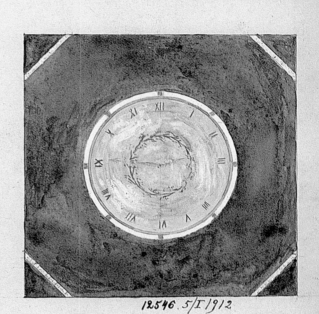

12546. 5/I 1912

12548 6/III 1912.

12338 нефр гу 15/VII 1911

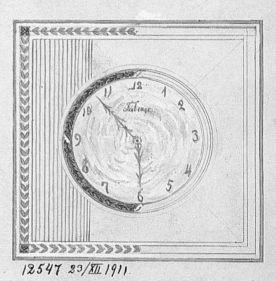

12547 23/XII 1911

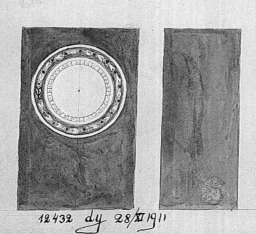

12432 dy 28/X 1911

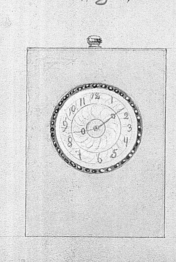

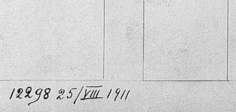

12298 25/VIII 1911

Chapter Five

Images of St. Petersburg
and the Art of Carl Fabergé

A purpurine table clock with a signed enamel dial bordered by a diamond-set gold wreath; it is similar to the example shown on plate 303.

Fabergé's roots in the decorative arts of eighteenth-century Western Europe have often received attention. Several well-documented examples illustrate this reverence for earlier Western work.[1] But this influence is much more than a stylistic and technical one, for the attraction of Russian society at the beginning of the twentieth century to this pinnacle of goldsmith work reveals much about life in Russia in the post-Petrine era. While an appetite for such Western art did exist, Fabergé did not merely create updated versions. Using these sources as a truly Russian artist, he played a critical role in the continuation of the work of Peter the Great,[2] incorporating the best of the West as in other areas of the Russian arts, both decorative and fine. Images of Peter's creation, the city of St. Petersburg, in the work of Carl Fabergé provide perhaps the finest illustration of this phenomenon, demonstrating the jeweler's integral role in the continuum of post-Petrine Russian art history.

The Wigström album presents a large collection of pieces produced by this great workmaster, over a relatively short stretch of time. We therefore have before us a cross-section of Fabergé's work for a defined period, and with it a unique opportunity to evaluate the firm in the context of both art and social history.[3] Fortunately for such an analysis, the period in question is perhaps among the most dynamic in the history of St. Petersburg and of Russia as a whole.

In the wake of the bicentenary of the founding of St. Petersburg in 1703 and the events of the Revolution of 1905, the period covers the rapid process of industrialization in the years before the Great War, and straddles not only the anniversary of the 1812 victory over Napoleon, but also the Romanov Tercentenary of 1913. It was thus a turbulent time that allowed great scope for the romanticization of Russia's past.

A table clock carved from a rectangular block of nephrite. Shown on plate 303, it is today in the Cleveland Museum of Art.

A table clock with striped black, pink and white enamel, purchased in London by Leopold de Rothschild (Pl. 303).

PLATE 303

Drawings of various table clocks in purpurine, hardstone, and enamel.

PLATE 309

Drawings of hardstone and enamel table clocks, including an elephant bearing a clock in the form of a howdah.

The monument to Peter the Great, one of the most powerful images of the new capital city, commissioned by Catherine the Great from the French sculptor Falconet in 1782.

Fabergé gave expression to his artistic talents through his beautiful combination of precious metals and precious stones, enamels, and hardstones. Only on a very few types of object does he incorporate external imagery, for example in the miniatures on plate 13 of the album, the religious works on plate 75, the portrait miniatures on the same plate, and a small number of other examples. Both within the album and outside it, Wigström's work contains numerous images of buildings and monuments, particularly from St. Petersburg. These depictions of the city are all the more striking when one considers the relatively small number of such images to be found among the works of Mikhail Perkhin, chief workmaster until 1903. Plate 135 of the Wigström album, for example, presents a rectangular box that features on its lid an image of the famous monument to Peter the Great in St. Petersburg (below), a tribute from Catherine the Great in 1782, created by the French sculptor Etienne-Maurice Falconet (1716-91).

Architectural imagery in eighteenth-century Europe

Images of architectural landmarks and monuments have taken many forms in the decorative arts. For Fabergé, the most important source was probably that eighteenth-century digest of all that was finest in the art of the goldsmith-jeweler: the snuffbox, with painted miniatures or *en camaïeu* enamel decoration. Fashionable at court and invaluable as important gifts, snuffboxes offered a wonderful vehicle for propaganda, in a form that was both precious and portable.

French boxes are the finest and the most numerous of the period, so the architectural scenes that do appear

Drawing of a cigarette case with a medallion depicting the statue of Peter the Great in St. Petersburg and illustrating its importance in the imagery of the city (Pl. 135).

12926 6/II 1912.

12861. 12.IV.1912 onig. 56° зол.
13135. 25.VI.1912 " 88⅔ сереб.

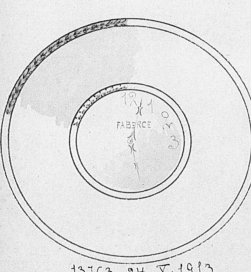

13763. 24.X.1913.

12568. 26.9.1912.

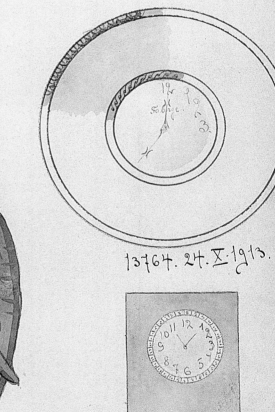

13764. 24.X.1913.

13311. 22.III.1913.

13780.17. Dek. 13.

13786. 4.X.1913.

№ 13254

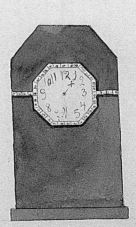

13734. 4.X. 1913.

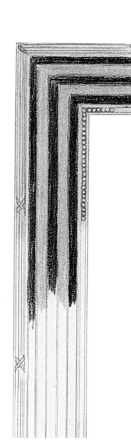

PLATE 329

Drawings of various frames for photographs, including one in gilded silver, gold and pink *guilloché* enamel, with the corresponding piece.

Drawing (detail) of a frame enameled with the colors (black and orange) of the order of St. George, featured on plate 315. A corresponding frame was purchased in London by Grand Duke Mikhail Alexandrovich in August 1911.

also tend to be French. The most famous of the French miniaturists who produced such scenes, especially in the 1760s and 1770s, are Louis-Nicolas and Henri-Joseph Van Blarenberghe, father and son. Snuffboxes with their work feature tableaux of contemporary events, as well as particularly significant sites in Paris. Miniatures in a box by Jean-Joseph Barrière, for example, depict French royal residences such as Versailles.[4] Louis-Nicolas Van Blarenberghe's portrait in miniature of the equestrian statue of Louis XV, and of its unveiling in 1763, presages later Russian images of Falconet's famous work.[5] The development of St. Petersburg in the eighteenth century was of sufficient renown also to merit treatment by Van Blarenberghe. A box now at Waddesdon Manor, made by Pierre-François Drais[6] in 1774, depicts scenes relating to the reign of Empress Catherine the Great of Russia, the lid and base featuring the feat required to transport and install the granite for the base of Falconet's statue. So momentous was this event that it appears on several other gold boxes, including one made for Catherine the Great herself.[7]

It is quite likely that Fabergé would have known the Van Blarenberghes' work, examples of which may still be seen in the Hermitage today. It could be argued, indeed, that such eighteenth-century boxes must certainly have provided direct inspiration. But it is more illuminating to consider Fabergé as a Russian artist, subject to all the associated forces at work in St. Petersburg at this time.

Comparably powerful Russian imagery had already appeared in Russian goldwork of the eighteenth century, contributing to the quasi-mythical status of St. Petersburg, and of its creator. Peter forcibly raised St. Petersburg from the swamps, determined

The fuchsia *guilloché* enamel table clock featured on plate 307: a popular form of clock.

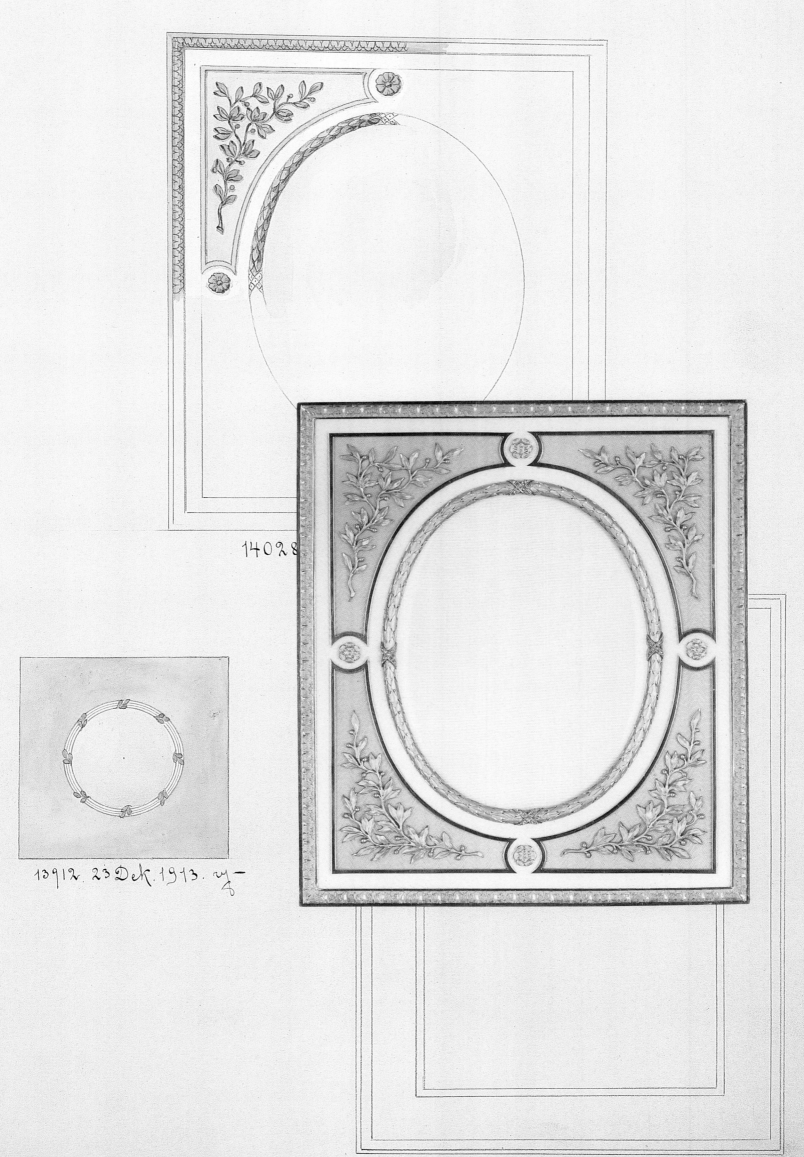

14028

13912. 23 Dek. 1913. cy–

14236. 22. Anb. 1913.

to build a capital to rival its Western counterparts. The arts, both fine and decorative, were able to capture, display, and disseminate the new city's landscapes and riverscapes, architecture, and monuments, all of which themselves both symbolized and institutionalized Peter's policy of Europeanization.[8] In a Russian culture that placed great importance on presentation gifts,[9] gold snuffboxes proved wonderful vehicles toward this end. At the same time, painted portrait miniatures were also popular under Peter the Great, so the leap from these to other types of miniature portrait was only a small one.

The beginnings of St. Petersburg imagery

Perhaps most renowned in the first rank of jewelers in Russia was the court goldsmith Jérémie Pauzié,[10] who in 1754, on the occasion of the baptism of Paul I, created a large gold sweetmeat box for Peter the Great's daughter Empress Elizabeth. This box features a monumental bust of Elizabeth, along with a view of the city behind a foreground of water and sailing craft.[11,12] Around 1770, Jean-Pierre Ador (d. 1784) created a box with enameled painted miniatures glorifying the events of Catherine the Great's reign, as a gift from the Empress to her favorite Grigori Orlov.[13,14] While the base depicts the "Apotheosis of Catherine", it is significant that the figure of the Empress, sounding a trumpet, is placed against the background of St. Petersburg's famed Peter-Paul Fortress. This structure, the city's first fortress, appears as early as 1704 in an engraving now in the Russian National Library.[15] The River Neva also features in this composition. Indeed water — conquered by Peter for the benefit of the city yet still a constant threat — figures prominently

A diptych frame in white *guilloché* enamel, the drawing for which appears on plate 333.

The desk of Grand Duchess Xenia Alexandrovna at Wilderness House. By the turn of the century, developments of photography ensured that portraits of loved ones were always at hand.

in most St. Petersburg imagery. The year 1782 saw the dedication of Falconet's statue, and soon afterwards the important Russian goldsmith Jean-François-Xavier Bouddé (d. 1789) created a box featuring the sculpture in enamel on the cover.[16] This statue constituted perhaps the most powerful symbol of Peter's work.[17]

In 1761, Pauzié created a four-color gold box as a gift from Elizabeth to the Imperial ambassador Count Nicholas Esterházy-Galantha, decorated with engraved and chased views of scenes in and around St. Petersburg, with the Peter-Paul Fortress again prominent, as well as the Admiralty. Significantly, these views were based on engravings of St. Petersburg made in 1753 and 1761 after Mikhail Makhaiev (1718-70),[18] for the earliest representations of St. Petersburg in the eighteenth century were actually to be found in the graphic arts and painting. Peter the Great had brought Europe's print revolution to Russia, thus providing a wonderful medium through which to disseminate his message. So strong was this message intended to be, as Kaganov points out,[19] that early depictions of the city were deliberately unconventional, serving to drive home a particular point of view rather than merely presenting simple portraits of buildings and monuments, as was so often the case with other European cityscapes. And in St. Petersburg, every structure portrayed had a certain mythical significance as well. Makhaiev's engravings were executed under the supervision of Giuseppe Valeriani, an experienced painter of panoramas from Venice, that other much-painted city offering obvious comparisons with St. Petersburg.

Drawing of an easel with a frame incorporating a miniature or a photograph, Fabergé's elegant variation on the theme of photograph frames (Pl. 337).

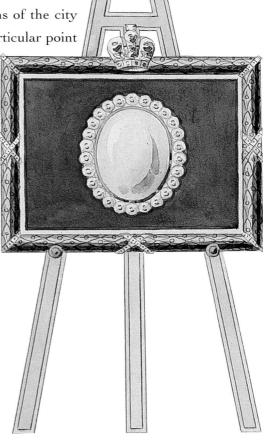

An oblong silver and
niello snuffbox depicting
Falconet's equestrian
statue of Peter the Great on
the cover (Moscow *c.*1825).

PLATE *377*

Drawings of a lady's desk
set in pale blue enamel
over a *guilloché* ground,
with ribbon-tied
rose garlands *en grisaille.*

Views of the city continued to proliferate throughout
the eighteenth century. When Giacomo Quarenghi
(1744-1817), its famous neo-classical architect, first
arrived there from Italy in 1779, he offered his own impressions of
St. Petersburg, soon to include drawings both of the Falconet statue, and of
the Peter-Paul Fortress.

Working at the turn of the nineteenth century, Feodor Yakovlevich
Alekseiev (1753/5-1824), who had studied in Venice and became known as
the Russian Canaletto, painted views of St. Petersburg in oils. He took his
inspiration in Russia from Hubert Robert (1733-1808), the French "pio-
neer of the cityscape, ...whose works were avidly collected by Catherine II,
Emperor Paul, and Alexander I..."[20] Other important artists working in
this genre were Semion Shchedrin (1745-1804), who painted predominantly palaces, and Benjamin Patersen, known for his graphics.[21]

Imagery in the nineteenth and early twentieth centuries

The beginning of the nineteenth century brought significant changes that
have a bearing upon our consideration of Fabergé. First came the further
enhancement of the myth of St. Petersburg, and the popularization of views
of the city by virtue of the development of lithography in Russia.

A porcelain wine cooler
from the Guriev Service
with views of St. Petersburg
in the reserves, here the
monument to Peter the Great;
from the collection of
the State Museum Reserve
Peterhof.

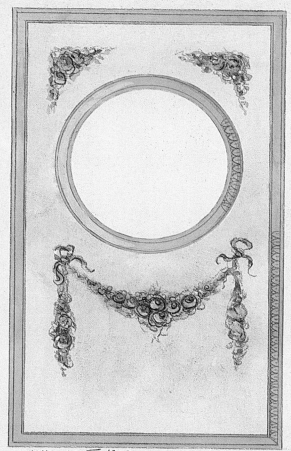

13140. 28. IV. 1912.

13092. 28. IV. 1912.

13084. 28. IV. 1912.

13085. 28. IV. 1912.

13086. 28. IV. 1912.

13082. 28. IV. 1912.

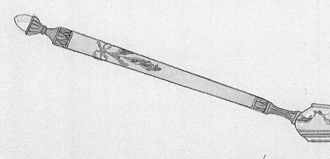

13083. 28/IV 1912.

12540 12/VIII 1911

12592, 11/I 1912 ed Прип.

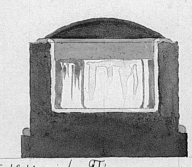

12594 11/I 1912. id Прип.

12589 11/I 1912. Прип. zd

12586 11/I 1912 Прип. dy

12593 pdy 11/I 1912 Прип.

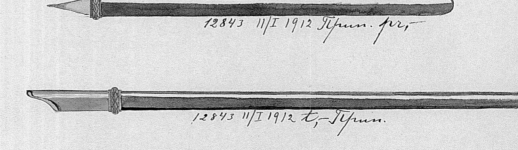

12843 11/I 1912 Прип. pr,

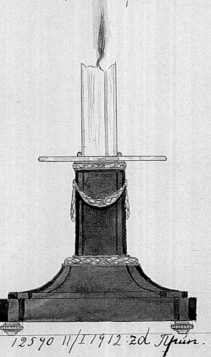

12590 11/I 1912. zd Прип.

12843 11/I 1912 t, Прип.

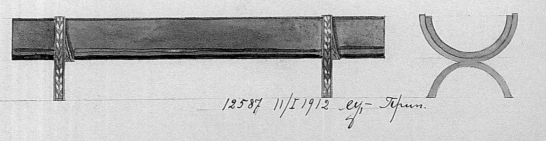

12587 11/I 1912 ey, Прип.

PLATE 379

Drawings of a rock crystal
inkwell and a desk set in
nephrite with gold mounts.

Compilations of such views were produced by this technique in the 1820s, at a selling price reasonable enough to render them widely accessible. Secondly, encouraged by this development, the "Empire Period" brought an increasing emphasis on the interior in daily life. Not only does the interior offer a private view out onto the world, but it also enables and encourages us to see the world in miniature, through the visual and decorative arts, and also through literature (Alexander Pushkin's poem *The Bronze Horseman* appeared in 1833). The process of internalization was to repeat itself a century later, during the period when Henrik Wigström was active,[22] in Russian homes that held the "memory books" so popular towards the end of the nineteenth century, featuring depictions of famous buildings and events.[23] Of particular significance in the elevation of St. Petersburg's reputation through lithography were images based on Vasily Sadovnikov's (1800-79) *Panorama*[24] of the Nevsky Prospect in the early 1830s. Nevsky Prospect was one of numerous projects undertaken in St. Petersburg at this time.

Drawing of a pink enamel
miniature column
with four revolving frames,
featured on plate 323.

Others of the decorative arts in the nineteenth century also contributed to the development and spread of the Petersburg myth. Silver boxes with niello decoration featuring views of St. Petersburg became widespread (see p.140). Lacquered papier-mâché boxes played a similar role, especially those produced by the Vishniakov Factory. The Imperial Porcelain Factory also favored views of St. Petersburg. A porcelain Easter egg from 1840, now in the Hermitage Museum, features the Admiralty with the Winter Palace Square in the background, based on an engraving,[25] while the Guriev (1809-17) and Babigon services (1823-4), among others, are both decorated with numerous views of St. Petersburg. A wine cooler, for example, features both Falconet's statue and the Peter-Paul Fortress (see p.140).[26] But while such views abounded, they did not constitute an architectural

A gold-mounted
nephrite taperstick used
for melting sealing wax,
part of the desk set
depicted on plate 379.

Drawing of a pill box
featuring a "landscape scene"
in moss agate, taken from
plate 203.

PLATE 381

Drawings of three
pieces from the desk set
shown on plate 379:
a desk lamp, a seal
and a stamp moistener.

inventory of the city, but were rather individual portraits of particular structures that embodied in some manner the myth of St. Petersburg.[27] When Vasili Ivanovich Surikov (1846-1916) arrived in St. Petersburg from Siberia, almost a century after Quarenghi, he too was immediately struck by the city, and in 1870 he painted his ghostly *Monument to Peter the Great in Senate Square in St. Petersburg*.[28] His work foreshadows the imagery of the "World of Art" movement, *Mir Iskusstva*, one of whose founders, A.N. Benois (1870-1960), was to illustrate Alexander Pushkin's *Bronze Horseman* in 1905. The centenary of Pushkin's birthday was celebrated in 1899, one year after the founding of *Mir Iskusstva*. Benois' frontispiece features Evgeni, the protagonist of the poem, fleeing from Peter the Great on horseback, casting an enormous shadow across the city.[29] Anna Petrovna Ostroumova-Lebedeva (1871-1955) and Mstislav Valerianovich Dobuzhinsky (1875-1957) contributed surreal views of St. Petersburg in the early twentieth century. *Mir Iskusstva* examined eighteenth- and early nineteenth-century Russian monuments in its efforts to explore Russian imagery in the context of contemporary European art. Benois himself was fascinated by the monuments of France, perhaps as a consequence of the Franco-Russian Alliance of the 1890s and the monuments that resulted from it, rooted in the ties between Louis XIV and Peter the Great.[30]

In evoking the past, the World of Art movement set out to protect St. Petersburg from the rapid development of the turbulent and threatening early twentieth century. The Petersburg cult gained new momentum at the beginning of the century, and strengthened after the Revolution of 1905.

Drawing of a box featuring
the Borodino Monument at
Tsarsköe Selo (Pl. 149), and
the actual monument today.

12591, 11/I 1912 d. Прип.

12588 11/I 1912 руу Прип.

12595 rd 11/I 1912 Прип.

Gold and enamel circular bonbonnière, featuring paintings in sepia enamel of St. Petersburg monuments (statues of Peter the Great — on the lid — and Catherine the Great — on the base).

The symbolic imagery of St. Petersburg now "had ripened for so long in the depth of Russian culture that by the beginning of the twentieth century, it was not so much that it was created as that it finally received its complete artistic expression..."[31] Nicholas II himself took no further part in the development of this symbolism, leaving it instead to artists and writers.[32]

Henrik Wigström

Workmaster Mikhail Perkhin died in 1903. Henrik Wigström succeeded him as chief workmaster, amid the turmoil of the early twentieth century and the renaissance of the Petersburg cult. Transforming the monumental into miniature form, accessible in intimate spaces, Wigström offered a perceived control over events, conveyed yet further through the function of these pieces as gifts.[33] Fabergé's precious objects lent themselves to such miniaturization and presentation, and Wigström's output included some of Petersburg's most famous structures in miniature. The many imperial and noble provenances for objects bearing St. Petersburg imagery are an indication of the mythical status of the city, of the need or desire to preserve that status, and of the comfort these images provided.

Falconet's statue, the Peter-Paul Fortress, and the Admiralty, which we have already seen on works of the eighteenth and nineteenth centuries, are found with particular frequency in Wigström's work. The British Royal Collection contains a box decorated with a *grisaille* and sepia enamel miniature of the Bronze Horseman, similar to the example shown on plate 135 of the album and described earlier (see p.134). Formerly in the collection of Prince Galitzin, the box may be dated from Zuiev's miniature to the Romanov Tercentenary year of

Circular gold-mounted rock crystal box, the cover featuring Falconet's statue of Peter the Great in sepia enamel; from the FORBES Magazine Collection, New York.

1913. A second rectangular box, also similar to the one on plate 135 of the album, features a sepia plaque of the statue: in about 1910, this box was presented to the Portuguese envoy by members of the St. Petersburg nobility (see p.61). A circular bonbonnière by Wigström again features the statue in sepia, in addition to the 1873 monument of Catherine the Great on its base (above): two of the most important figures in the history of St. Petersburg, and the two names inscribed on the base of Falconet's statue! From the collections of Empress Alexandra comes yet another Wigström image of the Horseman, in enamel on the cover of a box. And in the British Royal Collection, another similar box by Wigström features the Horseman on the lid, once again in tandem with another St. Petersburg image — this time the Peter-Paul Fortress in enamel on the base.[34] Plate 159 of the album presents a small circular box with enameled border, probably with another image of Peter the Great.

Not all Fabergé boxes with Falconet's statue were by Wigström, however, as demonstrated by Feodor Afanassiev's box in the British Royal Collection,[35] and by a cloisonné enamel box of Moscow manufacture from the same period as the album.[36] Fabergé depicted Falconet's statue in other media as well, including Rappoport's silver statue on a bowenite base in the Thai Royal Collection,[37] or on a rhodonite base,[38] in a similar fashion to the numerous nineteenth-century bronzes of Peter set on malachite or lapis lazuli bases.

Certainly the impending anniversary of St. Petersburg in 1903 must have inspired Perkhin's miniature version of the statue on an emerald base from the collection of Mikhailovsky actress Elisabeth (Elisa) Balletta (now in the Hillwood Museum), as well as the surprise set on a sapphire base contained in the 1903 Imperial Peter the Great Easter egg (right).[39]

The surprise concealed in the Peter the Great Imperial Easter egg of 1903: a miniature statue of Falconet's monument in gold and sapphire; Virginia Museum of Fine Arts, Bequest of Lillian Thomas Pratt.

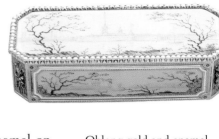

Oblong gold and enamel
box with the Peter-Paul
Fortress and landscape views
painted in sepia enamel;
from the FORBES Magazine
Collection, New York.

Oval gold, pink and sepia
enamel snuffbox,
the cover depicting the
Peter-Paul Fortress,
workmaster Mikhail Perkhin.

The Peter-Paul Fortress appears in painted enamel on several of Fabergé's boxes, including one by Wigström (now in the FORBES Magazine Collection) showing the fortress as viewed from across the Neva (right). Perkhin's oval box features a similar view of the fortress in pink and sepia enamel, with views of the Neva on its sides and base (left). Crossing to the opposite bank of the Neva for another over-the-water view, plate 201 of the album shows a nephrite box from 1911 bearing a view of St. Isaac's Cathedral, with boats in the foreground (see p.93). You can almost see the famous equestrian statue, while to the left is the Admiralty (built in 1806) — a building which is also prominent, in sepia and blue enamel, on Wigström's clock (opposite). Other views of St. Petersburg were also depicted, including (it is presumed) the example on plate 217 of the album. Enamel was not the only medium employed for these miniature landscapes. Wigström's snuffbox,[40] for example (opposite), features miniatures of the Summer Palace complex at Peterhof, founded about 200 years earlier, in 1714, by Peter the Great. Monuments represented in miniature by Wigström frequently have connections with specific St. Petersburg figures, such as the Yusupov Palaces enamel music box (now in the Hillwood Museum), presented by Prince Felix Felixovich Yusupov to his parents in 1907 to commemorate their twenty-fifth wedding anniversary. The Chernyshev Bridge and the Ministry of the Interior, meanwhile, appear on a frame made in 1906, presented to a high-ranking Ministry official and now in the State Hermitage Museum.[41]

Wigström used the same pink and sepia enamel technique to depict monuments

View of the Peter-Paul
Fortress erected
at the command of Peter
the Great in 1703 and
marking the foundation
of his new capital.

The Admiralty originally enclosed the shipyards so vital to the development of St. Petersburg. It was rebuilt at the beginning of the nineteenth century by the architect Andrei Zakharov.

Oval gold and enamel snuffbox, set with painted miniatures of Peterhof — here the Great Palace, from the collection of the State Museum Reserve Peterhof.

outside Russia as well. On plate 219 of the album, we see the side of a nephrite box from the Royal Collection, Thailand, the top of which features the Temple of Dawn (see p.110).[42] Another nephrite box in the same collection features the Chakri Palace in sepia.[43] Fabergé's English clients were especially fond of such scenes: in 1911, Princess Victoria purchased a frame by Wigström on which he depicted the dairy at Sandringham, while Windsor and Balmoral appear on a Wigström bonbonnière, Hampton Court on another frame of the period, and Chatsworth on a Louis XVI-style Wigström snuffbox commissioned by the Duke of Devonshire.[44]

As mentioned earlier, Wigström was active during a momentous period in Russian history. The equestrian figure of Alexander III on the Imperial Egg in the Kremlin dating from 1910 "commemorates the unveiling in St. Petersburg in the same year of an equestrian figure of Alexander III made by Paul Troubetzkoy."[45] The miniature column of Alexander on plate 165 of the album (see p.76) was completed on 13 September 1912,[46] and in the same year a statue of Alexander III was unveiled in Moscow. On plate 149 of the album, on a small box finished on 28 August 1912, there appears a columned monument from Tsarsköe Selo commemorating the Borodino celebrations that took place in late August and early September (see p.144). This box relates to the album's only Imperial Easter egg, the Napoleonic Egg on plate 189, which commemorated the Russian victory over Napoleon in 1812 in an effort to encourage Russian patriotism.[47]

Gold-mounted blue *guilloché* enamel clock with a sepia view of the Admiralty in St. Petersburg.

6 14 Экат
110 р.

11118 18 VII 1912

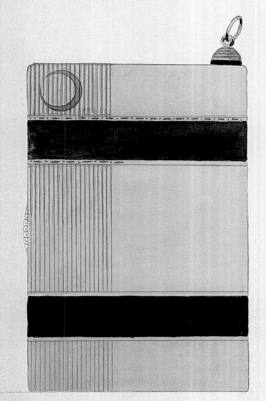

№ 13420
-4 ДЕК 1912

№ 13405
24 НОЯ 1911

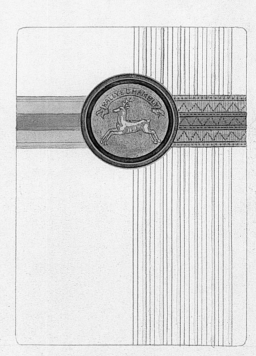

№ 13434
-4 ДЕК 1912

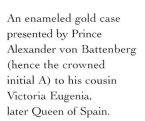

An enameled gold case
presented by Prince
Alexander von Battenberg
(hence the crowned
initial A) to his cousin
Victoria Eugenia,
later Queen of Spain.

A signed photograph of
Princess Cécile Murat, one
of Fabergé' most flamboyant
customers, painted
by John Singer Sargent.

PLATE 400

Drawings of cigarette
cases in gold and enamel.
Two of them were
commissioned by Princess
Cécile Murat, including
one for the *Rallye Chambly*,
the Murat family stag hunt.

The Imperial Easter eggs bear a great number of views of St. Petersburg, and by their very creation and presentation may themselves be considered monuments of the period.[48] Most notable in this context is perhaps Perkhin's Peter the Great egg of 1903, decorated with miniatures showing the development of St. Petersburg, from Peter's log hut to the Winter Palace. Perkhin also created the Pelican Egg of 1897, showing educational institutions for women of privilege; the Easter egg of 1896, featuring Imperial residences; and another egg in 1901 depicting the Gatchina Palace. Wigström contributed the Alexander Palace Egg of 1908, and the Fifteenth Anniversary Egg of 1911, with miniatures depicting the major events of Nicholas II's reign. Each of these symbolic and elaborate presentation pieces made use of St. Petersburg imagery to telling effect, endowing that imagery with greater legitimacy in the process.

Through the work of Henrik Wigström, Fabergé thus brought to its culmination a process begun by Peter the Great. The imagery of St. Petersburg that appears in many of these objects is not merely a twentieth-century version of eighteenth-century subjects, nor is it simply a souvenir of the scenes depicted. As a Russian artist, Fabergé was both subject to, and part of, the forces shaping the advance of Russian art history. He contributed to the development of the symbolism and significance of the city of his birth and residence, in a period that offered rich opportunities in this field. The images of St. Petersburg represented in this album are very specific, forceful in meaning, and repeated many times. These precious objects thus enabled a powerful message to be disseminated in a manner that is both tangible and beautiful, as befits the legacy of Peter the Great.

A photograph of Queen
Victoria Eugenia of Spain,
née Battenberg.

A cigarette case in gold
and black polished enamel,
presented to Charles
Luzarche d'Azay
by Princess Cécile Murat
on New Year's Day 1913.

CHAPTER I. HENRIK WIGSTRÖM

Notes

1. A. Kenneth Snowman, the doyen of Fabergé research, discovered the Holmström stock books. *See* Snowman, 1993.

2. *See* Fabergé et al., 1992. This publication includes the recollections of Franz P. Birbaum, head designer at Fabergé. Birbaum's manuscript was found by Valentin Skurlov, the St. Petersburg Fabergé researcher, among the papers of the mineralogist A.E. Fersman in Moscow.

3. Bainbridge, 1949, p.121. Henry C. Bainbridge was Fabergé's representative in London from 1908 to 1917.

4. Ibid., p.125.

5. Finland was a Grand Duchy of imperial Russia in the years 1809-1918. Although technically a part of the Empire, the country enjoyed a high degree of autonomy, so travel documents were required for shorter or longer sojourns in Russia.

6. St. Petersburg offered a ready market for the farmers of southern Finland. Their carts provided an inexpensive means of transport for the thousands of young girls and boys seeking positions in the capital — the girls mostly as domestic servants and the boys as craft apprentices. *See* Engman, 1983.

7. Carl Fabergé's younger brother Agathon (1862-1895) was his close assistant, and a brilliant and innovative designer. The early success of the family business owed much to his talents.

8. Information from the unpublished annual reports of Alexander Tillander. Two generations of the Tillander family owned a retail store with its own workshops in St. Petersburg. They were suppliers, albeit on a small scale, to the Office of His Imperial Majesty. The business, founded in 1860, reopened after the Revolution in Helsinki, Finland.

9. In 1896, Fabergé employed a total of 476 people, including 31 apprentices. Information from Will Lowes, Fabergé sales catalog researcher.

10. The Gold- and Silversmiths' Guild system, based on the German model, was introduced into St. Petersburg in 1714. The craftsmen who first settled in St. Petersburg after the foundation of the city in 1703 were principally of German origin. Following the German guild tradition, and perhaps as a pretext for getting together in a national group, these masters combined into a guild of their own, although this had no legal basis. The Russian goldsmiths of St. Petersburg followed their example the same year, resulting in two guilds, one for foreign masters and the other for their Russian counterparts. In 1721 the guilds were given official recognition.

11. The information on the plan of the Fabergé building complex is based on old photographs, research of the building itself, and on fragmentary information from various sources.

12. Hjalmar Armfelt (1873-1959), a Finn, specialized in the making of useful objects such as frames, writing implements, etc. Finnish-born August Hollming (1854-1913) and his son Wäinö (1885-1934), were makers of cigarette cases and small gold jewelry. Likewise, Finnish-born August Holmström (1829-1903) and his son Albert (1876-1925) specialized in gem-set fine jewelry. Three of the Imperial Easter eggs were made in their workshop. Alfred Thielemann (d. *c.*1910) and his son Karl Rudolf were makers of commemorative *jetons*, badges, and small gold jewelry.

The makers of the holly-wood cases in which every object made at Fabergé was sold were important to the House. Each case was hand-made and fitted individually to the piece that it enclosed. The Fabergé case-makers, Käki, Kämärä, and Ampuja, were of Finnish origin.

13. Information from the manuscript memoirs of Jalmari Haikonen, an engraver at the Wigström workshop from 1915 to 1918.

14. Information from the memoirs of Jalmari Haikonen. The snuffbox was a gift for the sixtieth birthday of the former Commander-in-Chief, Grand Duke Nikolai Nikolaievich.

15. Stefan Wäkevä and Alexander Tillander, for example, were ten and eleven respectively when first apprenticed. *See* Tillander-Godenhielm, 1980, p.49.

16. Information from Anni Sarvi, Henrik Wigström's granddaughter.

17. Information from Helmi Polvinen, daughter of the goldsmith master Tuomas Polvinen, workmaster to the jeweler Julius Butz. Helmi Polvinen was a playmate of the Wigström children, who visited them almost daily.

18. From the memoirs of Jalmari Haikonen.

19. *See* Aarne, 1945, pp.619-20 and the annotated designs of goldsmith master Tuomas Polvinen, workmaster to Julius Butz. The following are examples of the common vocabulary: *munderu*, to assemble, from the French verb *monter*; *justeera*, to adjust, from the German *justieren*; *fuga*, to join, from the German *fugen*; *spetspora*, a drill, from the German *Spitzbohr*; *martlee*, hammer, or hammered surface, from the French *marteau, marteler*; *Slippuu* or *polera*, to polish, from the German *schleifen* and *polieren; and lufti*, an open setting, from the German *Luft*.

20. Information from Helmi Polvinen.

21. Information from Lyyli Wigström. For further information on the Imperial Coronation Egg, *see* Fabergé et al., 1997, pp.130-2. The Coronation Egg is part of the Forbes Collection, New York. *See* Forbes, et al., 1999, pp.36-9.

22. Information from the memoirs of Jalmari Haikonen.

23. Ibid.

24. Information on Rutsch as a subcontractor from Valentin Skurlov.

25. Fabergé et al., 1992, p.46.

26. The hardstone parts of the objects shown throughout the album are marked with a price code for the purpose of invoicing between the workshops of Kremlev and Wigström. The code has been deciphered by Valentin Skurlov. The Latin letter P corresponds to 1, R to 2, Z to 3, E to 4, D to 5, M to 6, I to 7, A to 8, T to 9 and Y to 0. Thus the coded price ZDY for the nephrite kovsh on plate 263 of the album was equivalent to 350 roubles.

27. According to Fabergé et al., 1992, p.50, Nikolai A. Petrov was the enameling master at Fabergé from 1895 to 1917. He was the son of Alexander F. Petrov, a Moscow artisan who taught both his sons the art of enameling.

28. Information from the memoirs of Jalmari Haikonen.

29. Ibid.

30. The Grand Duchy of Finland declared itself an independent republic in 1918.

31. Anni Sarvi.

Bibliography

Books and articles:

AARNE, Uuno V., ed. Kultasepän Käsikirja, SKS, Helsinki, 1945.

BAINBRIDGE, Henry Charles. Peter Carl Fabergé, B.T.Batsford Ltd., London, 1949.

ENGMAN, Max. S:t Petersburg och Finland. Migration och influens 1703-1917, Helsingfors, 1983.

FABERGÉ, Tatiana et al. The History of the House of Fabergé. (Includes the memoirs of Franz P. Birbaum), Russkiye Samotsvety, St. Petersburg, 1992.

FABERGÉ, TATIANA ET AL. The Fabergé Imperial Easter Eggs, Christie's, London, 1997.

FORBES, Christopher et al. FABERGÉ, The Forbes Collection, Hugh Lauter Levin Associates, Inc., 1999.

TILLANDER-GODENHIELM. 1980. "Personal and Historical Notes on Fabergé's Finnish Workmasters and Designers" in Carl Fabergé and His Contemporaries, Tieto, Helsinki, 1980.

Unpublished sources

HAIKONEN, Jalmari, Lappeenranta, Finland. Memoirs. The Haikonen family.

POLVINEN, Helmi, Helsinki, Finland. Recollections. The Polvinen family archive.

POLVINEN, Tuomas, St. Petersburg, Russia. Design albums. The Polvinen family archive.

TILLANDER, Alexander T., St. Petersburg, Russia. Annual reports of the company. The Tillander family archive.

Information from the following individuals

LOWES, Will, Fabergé sales catalog researcher, Adelaide, Australia.

McCANLESS, Christel L., library consultant, Huntsville, Alabama. U.S.A.

SARVI, ANNi, granddaughter of Henrik Wigström, Helsinki, Finland.

SKURLOV, Valentin, Fabergé researcher, St. Petersburg, Russia.

WIGSTRÖM, Lyyli, daughter of Henrik Wigström, Västanfjärd, Finland.

CHAPTER II. PATRONS OF PRESTIGE

Notes

1. *See* the chapter by Peter L. Schaffer in the present book.

2. For further information on imperial presentation gifts, *see* Schaffer, 1997.

In Fabergé et al, 1992, p.30, there is a revealing description of the manner in which imperial commissions were handled at the Office of His Imperial Majesty. At the time under discussion (1912-14) Lieutenant-General Evgeni Nikolaevich Volkov was head of the Office and Count Vladimir Borisovich Freederickz was Minister of the Court. The elderly and over-worked Court Minister could not possibly have given his attention to decisions of this nature. This publication includes the recollections of Franz P. Birbaum, head designer at Fabergé. Birbaum's manuscript was found by Valentin Skurlov, the St. Petersburg Fabergé researcher, among the papers of the mineralogist A.E. Fersman in Moscow. The recollections contain information concerning the way in which the firm of Fabergé was organized and managed.

3. The "Table of Ranks", first instituted by Peter the Great in 1724, consisted of fourteen ranks. The highest was Chancellor. A Serving Privy Councillor held rank II, while a person of rank XIV bore the title of Collegiate Registrar, familiar from Russian novels and short stories.

4. During the reign of Nicholas II, the accounts of the Office of His Imperial Majesty list 44 snuffboxes bearing the miniature portrait of the sovereign, 26 of which were supplied by Fabergé. The rest were made by the other court jewellers: 11 by G.A. Hahn, 5 by C.E. Bolin and 2 by F. Koechly. Prices vary between 1,500 and 4,500 roubles. *See* Tatiana Fabergé's annotations to lot 420 of Sotheby's, Geneva, 16-17 November 1998.

5. Of some 300 snuffboxes with the Emperor's diamond-set cipher, 150 were made by Fabergé. Fifty were made by Court Jeweler G.A. Hahn, 30 by F. Koechly, 30 by C.E. Bolin and perhaps 3 by A.D. Ivanov. Research on imperial presentation objects is currently being undertaken by Valentin Skurlov: this information comes from his findings. For an example of a snuffbox with a cipher and a known provenance, see Valentin Skurlov's annotations to lot 96 in Christie's, NewYork, 20 November 1999.

6. Tobacco, in the form of the *papirosa*, forerunner of the cigarette, was first introduced to Russia in the 1860s, following the Crimean War. The first boxes in precious metal by Fabergé to hold these new stimulants were produced in the early 1880s. See Traina, 1998, pp.25-8. The early cigarette boxes were fairly large, as they were fitted with tinder cords and compartments for matches. By 1910, when the lighter had been invented and the cigarette itself given its modern form, the cases were transformed into slim and elegant objects.

7. General Lukomsky's important function may have influenced the Emperor to increase the value of the presentation gift. Fabergé's original price on the case was 1,000 roubles. The case was then sent for alteration to the Court Supplier Ivan Morosov, who added diamonds to the value of 1,350 roubles. General Lukomsky's gift was therefore worth a total of 2,350 roubles. Information from Valentin Skurlov.

8. Information on this train journey comes from the unpublished memoirs of Axel von Weissenberg. *See* as well Skurlov et al, 1998, pp.182-8. Presentation gifts for people in subordinate positions included rings, cufflinks, studs, tie pins set with the Emperor's or Empress's cipher or the double-headed eagle, a variety of silver objects and watches decorated with the imperial coat of arms, most often manufactured by Pavel Buhré.

9. For more information on these early presentation objects, *see* von Solodkoff, 1981, pp.84-7.

10. One of the miniaturists working for Fabergé in the 1910s was Alexander Blaznov, who is known to have painted innumerable miniature portraits of the Emperor for official decorations and presentation snuffboxes. With his wife, Marie Paets-Blaznov, he painted the iconostasis of the New Church at Kronstadt. *See* Tillander-Godenhielm, 1996, pp.164-5.

11. *See* Marina Lopato's research into the accounts of the Office of His Imperial Majesty, in Habsburg et al., 1993, pp.58-61.

12. A badge (in Russian terms) is an emblem of a school or regiment or organization of some kind. It was usually made of silver or gold and enamel, with a post or nut on the back to attach it to a uniform. A *jeton* is a smaller object, what in the West used to be called a fob, also made out of silver or gold and enamel, emblematic of a school or regiment or other organization. It was suspended from a small chain, which was hung over a button. Badges were worn on the lower left breast, *jetons* near the upper right breast, usually just below the collar-bone. Information from Marvin Lyons.

13. Students of the Imperial Law School.

14. Information from Marvin Lyons.

15. The tradition was begun by Alexander III in 1885, and after his death, his son Nicholas II continued the custom of presenting an egg by Fabergé both to his mother and to his wife. For more information on the eggs and the tradition, *see* Fabergé et al., 1997.

In Fabergé et al., 1992, p.24, Birbaum asserts that his designs did not have to be submitted to the Emperor, that Carl Fabergé and his designers were free to decide on them themselves. This does not preclude the original "philosophy" behind these gifts: that each of them should include symbols of personal importance and meaning to the recipient.

16. For more information concerning the Imperial egg, *see* Fabergé et al., 1997, p.202.

17. Bainbridge, 1949, p.112. H.C. Bainbridge was Fabergé's representative in London from 1908 to 1917. He visited his employer and the House of Fabergé in St. Petersburg on a regular basis.

18. Ibid. and Skurlov, 1997, p.37.

19. Information from Valentin Skurlov, Alexei N. Guzanov, Head Curator of the State Pavlovsk Palace Museum, Russia and Refat Gafifullin, Curator of the Archives of the State Pavlovsk Palace Museum, Russia.

20. Skurlov, 1997, p.37.

21. Pridvornyi Kalendar (Court Calendar), 1912.

22. The Order of St. George could only be won through personal bravery in battle.

23. Information from Valentin Skurlov.

24. Grand Duke Dmitri Pavlovich inherited everything left by his assassinated uncle Grand Duke Sergei Alexandrovich.

25. Information from Marvin Lyons.

26. Victoria Melita of Saxe-Coburg-Gotha (1876-1936), known as Ducky, was the granddaughter of both Emperor Alexander II of Russia and Queen Victoria of England. She divorced her first husband, Grand Duke Ernst Ludwig of Hesse-Darmstadt, brother of Empress Alexandra Feodorovna, to marry her cousin, Grand Duke Kirill Vladimirovich.

27. Story related by Prince Dmitri Alexandrovich to Marvin Lyons.

28. Information from Marilyn Pfeifer Swezey, specialist in Russian decorative arts and cultural history.

29. Fabergé's London ledgers for the years 1906-17 are in the archive collections of Tatiana Fabergé, great granddaughter of Carl Fabergé. Information from these ledgers is quoted with the permission of Tatiana Fabergé.

30. Crawford et al., 1997, p.189.

31. Bing, 1937, p.283.

32. Grand Duke Sergei Mikhailovich (1869-1918) was a grandson of Nicholas I. He was the cousin of Alexander III.

33. Romanovsky-Krassinsky, 1960, pp.246-7.

34. Fabergé et al., 1992, p.28.

35. Information from Marvin Lyons. The families are listed in Mandich et al., 1992, the reprint of the *Gerbovnik*, pp.572, 582, 592 and 682.

36. Among them an exquisite music box set with six sepia enamel panels depicting the Yusupov palaces: a gift from the two sons on their parents' silver wedding anniversary in 1907. It is now in the Hillwood Museum, Washington, D.C. A flower composition — a cornflower with oat sprays — is now in the State Hermitage Museum, St. Petersburg.

37. Birbaum notes that, up to the 1890s, Russian clients were subject to a "blind worship of everything that was foreign…". Fabergé et al., 1992, p.24.

38. *See* Stolitsa i Usadba, 1914, no 5, 1 March, p.9. Nadelhoffer, 1984, p.131.

39. *See* Channon, 1995, p.78. In 1913, the net inflow of foreign investment was 578 million roubles, representing some 25 percent of net domestic investment.

40. van Gilse van der Pals, 1965, passim.

41. Tolf, 1977, passim.

42. Fabergé et al, 1992, pp.31-2.

43. Ibid.

44. For the story of how these designs came about, *see* Snowman, 1993, pp.24-6. The stock books of the Holmström workshop, in the archive collections of Wartski, London, show the whole range of Alma Pihl's designs.

45. Fabergé et al, 1997, pp.70-7.

46. Fabergé et al., 1992, p.32 and Bainbridge, 1949, p.8.

47. Romanovsky-Krassinsky, 1960, p.140.

48. Grand Duke Alexei Alexandrovich (1850-1908), son of Alexander II, was General-Admiral and Supreme Chief of the Russian Imperial Fleet.

49. *See* A La Vieille Russie, 1983, catalog nos. 309 and 442 also Forbes, 1999, pp.92-3. Information concerning Elisabeth Balletta was provided by Yulia Rybakova, Curator of Photography Department and Anna Shoulgat, Assistant to the Director of the St. Petersburg State Museum of Theatre and Music. Archive information on Mlle Balletta was provided by Valentin Skurlov.

50. Information concerning Lina Cavalieri was provided by Dr. Marina Godlevskaya, Head of the Opera Department and Photography Department of the St. Petersburg State Museum of Theatre and Music, and by Anna Shoulgat.

51. There are several references to Mlle Cavalieri in Nadelhoffer, 1984, pp.70, 75 and 233. In the London ledgers of Fabergé, Mlle Cavalieri is listed among the names of clients. Information from Tatiana Fabergé. *See* also Cavalieri, 1936.

52. Information on Anastasia Vialtseva was provided by Elina Samkova, Head of the Rare Books Department at the St. Petersburg State Museum of Theatre and Music, and by Anna Shoulgat.

53. Bainbridge, 1949, p.79. *See* also Snowman, 1953, p.52.

54. Ibid., pp.101-4.

55. Information from Tatiana Fabergé.

56. Ibid.

57. Princess Cécile Murat, (1867-1960), *née* Ney d'Elchingen, was a descendant of the celebrated Field Marshal Michel Ney, Duc d'Elchingen, Prince de La Moskowa and one of Napoleon's heroes from the campaign against Russia. The Princess was married to Joachim, 5th Prince Murat, who likewise had a Bonapartist background.

58. Joensuu, 1935. Interview with Agathon K. Fabergé. One million Finnish marks in the year 1935 equaled approximately US\$ 2,500. For a comparison with the actual prices, see below.

59. Interview with M. X. by Emmanuel Ducamp in Paris, September, 1999.

Bibliography

Books and articles:
A LA VIEILLE RUSSIE. *Fabergé, A Loan Exhibition*. Catalog of an exhibition at A La Vieille Russie, New York, 1983.
BAINBRIDGE, Henry Charles. *Peter Carl Fabergé*, B.T.Batsford Ltd., London, 1949.
BING, Edward J., ed. *The Letters of Tsar Nicholas and Empress Marie*, Ivor Nicholson and Watson Limited, London, 1937.
CAVALIERI, Lina. *Le mie verita*, Roma, 1936.
CHANNON, John et al. *The Penguin Historical Atlas of Russia*, London, 1995.
Christie's, New York, April 15, 1997.
Christie's, New York, November 20, 1999.
CRAWFORD, Rosemary et al. *Michael and Natasha. The Life and Love of Michael II, the Last of the Romanov Tsars*, A Lisa Drew Book/Scribner, New York, 1997.
FABERGÉ, Tatiana et al. *The History of the House of Fabergé*. (Includes the memoirs of Franz P. Birbaum), Russkiye Samotsvety, St. Petersburg, 1992.
FABERGÉ, Tatiana et al. *Fabergé and the St. Petersburg Jewellers* (in Russian), Neva, St. Petersburg, 1997.
FABERGÉ, Tatiana et al. *The Fabergé Imperial Easter Eggs*, Christie, Manson and Woods, Ltd., London, 1997.
Fabergé. A catalog of an exhibition at the Queen's Gallery, Buckingham Palace, London, 1955.
FORBES, Christopher et al. *Fabergé, The Forbes Collection*, Hugh Lauter Levin Associates, Inc., 1999.
VAN GILSE VAN DER PALS, Max H. *Levnadsminnen*, (Memories of My Life), Helsingfors, 1965.
VON HABSBURG, Géza et al. *Fabergé: Imperial Jeweler*, Abrams, New York, 1994.
JOENSUU, Väinö. "Kultainen joutsen ui akvamariinilaineilla" (A Swan of Gold on Waves of Aquamarine). Interview with Agathon K. Fabergé in the weekly journal *Suomen Kuvalehti*, no. 18, Helsinki, 1935.
MANDICH, Donald R. et al. *Russian Heraldry and Nobility*, Dramco Publishers, U.S.A., 1992.
A revised edition of the *Gerbovnik* [General Armorial of the Noble Families of the Russian Empire] published by the Russian Government serially from 1797 until 1840.
NADELHOFFER, Hans. *Cartier*, Editions du Regard, Paris, 1984.
Pridvornyi Kalendar, 1912. (Court Calendar of Imperial Russia).
ROMANOVSKY-KRASSINSKY, Mathilde. *Souvenirs de Kschessinska*, Librairie Plon, Paris, 1960.
SCHAFFER, Paul. "The Art of Giving. The Presentation Piece in Russian Decorative Arts". Catalog of the *International Fine Arts and Antique Dealers Show*, New York, 1997.
SKURLOV, Valentin. "Boris Frödman-Cluzel, Fabergé's Master Sculptor and New Light on Fabergé's Hardstone Figures" in *Carl Fabergé: Goldsmith to the Tsar*, Nationalmuseum, Stockholm, 1997.
SKURLOV, Valentin et al. "Keisarilliset tuliaiset" (Imperial Gifts) in *Keisarin Juna. Romanovit Suomen Rautateillä* (The Emperor's Train. The Romanovs on the Finnish Railways). The Finnish Railway Museum, Vammalan Kirjapaino, Vammala, 1998.
SNOWMAN, A. Kenneth. *The Art of Carl Fabergé*, Faber and Faber Limited, London, 1953.
SNOWMAN, A. Kenneth. *Fabergé: Lost and Found, The*

Recently Discovered Jewelry Designs from the St. Petersburg Archives. Abrams, New York, 1993.
VON SOLODKOFF, Alexander. *Russian Gold and Silver*. Trefoil Books Ltd, London, 1981.
Stolitsa i Usadba, (Town and Country), No 5, March 1, Petrograd, 1914.
Sotheby's, Geneva, November 16-7, 1998.
TILLANDER-GODENHIELM, Ulla. "Personal and Historical Notes on Fabergé's Finnish Workmasters and Designers." in *Carl Fabergé and His Contemporaries*, Tieto, Helsinki, 1980.
TILLANDER-GODENHIELM, Ulla. *Smycken från det Kejserliga St. Petersburg*, (Jewelry from Imperial St. Petersburg), Hagelstam, Helsingfors, 1996.
TOLF, Robert W. *The Russian Rockefellers*, Stockholm, 1977.
TRAINA, John. *The Fabergé Case, From the Private Collection of John Traina*, Abrams, New York, 1998.
WOLFF, M.O., Société, ed. *Almanach de St-Pétersbourg, Cour Monde et Ville*, St-Pétersbourg, 1912.

Unpublished sources:
Lowes and McCanless Index to Fabergé at Auction. (Manuscript). VON WEISSENBERG, AXEL, Helsinki, Finland. Memoirs. The von Weissenberg family archive.

Information from the following individuals:
DUCAMP, Emmanuel, Paris, France. Interview with M. X., a friend of Charles Luzarche d'Azay.
FABERGÉ, Tatiana, Versonnex, France.
GAFIFULLIN, Refat, Curator of the Archives of the State Pavlovsk Palace Museum, Russia.
GODLEVSKAYA, Marina, Head of Opera Department and Photography Department of St. Petersburg State Museum of Theatre and Music, St. Petersburg, Russia.
GUZANOV, Alexei N., Head Curator of the State Pavlovsk Palace Museum, Russia.
LOWES, Will, Fabergé sales catalogue researcher, Adelaide, Australia.
LYONS Marvin, historian and specialist in imperial Russian society, social and military institutions, Vancouver, Canada.
MCCANLESS, Christel L., library consultant, Huntsville, Alabama, U.S.A.
PFEIFER SWEZEY, Marilyn, specialist in Russian decorative arts and cultural history, Washington D.C., U.S.A.
RUBAKOVA, Yulia, Curator of Photography Department of St. Petersburg State Museum of Theatre and Music, St. Petersburg, Russia.
SAMKOVA, Elina, Head of Rare Books Department of St. Petersburg State Museum of Theatre and Music, St. Petersburg, Russia.
SHOULGAT, Anna, Assistant to the Director of St. Petersburg State Museum of Theatre and Music, St. Petersburg, Russia.
SKURLOV, Valentin, Fabergé researcher, St. Petersburg, Russia.

CHAPTER IV. THE TRIUMPH OF STYLE

Notes

1. Vanderbilt-Balsan, 1953, p.125.
2. Fabergé et al., 1992, p.7.
3. Ibid., p.46
4. "Artquake" is the term used by the early 20th century art critic, Desmond MacCarthy in Sunday

paper magazine.
5. Solvychegodsk, center of enamelwork in Northern Russia, late 17th century.
6. *World Exhibitions and Russian Exhibits*, St. Petersburg, 1886, p.1449.
7. *Kovsh* is a presentation bowl derived from the Russian peasant's ladle.
8. The Monomakh crown is the earliest crown of the Russian tsars, derived from Byzantium.
9. Nadelhoffer, 1984, p.142.
10. Notes by Mariano Fortuny y Madraz, Rome, December 12, 1937, during a visit to an inauguration of textiles on November 18, 1937. *Oggettivazione* – Italian translation.
11. Fabergé et al., 1992, p.4.
12. Nadelhoffer, 1984, pp.87.
13. Kostjuk, 1996, p.96.
14. Fabergé, 1992, p.42.

Bibliography

Books and articles
FABERGÉ, TATIANA ET AL. *The History of the House of Fabergé*. (includes the memoirs of Franz P. Birbaum), Russkiye Samotsvety, St. Petersburg, 1992.
KOSTIUK, OLGA G. ET AL. "100 Treasures of goldsmith's art of the Hermitage, St. Petersburg." in *Gold of the Tsars*, Arnoldsche, Stuttgart, 1996.
NADELHOFFER, HANS. *Cartier*, Editions du Regard, Paris, 1984.
'Seta e Oro – La collezione di tessuti di Mariano Fortuny'. (Silk and Gold – Mariano Fortuny's Collection of Fabrics). Exhibition at Biblioteca Nazionale Marciana, Venice, 1997-98
World Exhibition and Russian Exhibits, St. Petersburg, 1886.

CHAPTER V. IMAGES OF ST. PETERSBURG

Notes

1. For example, Julius Rappoport's silver and bowenite clock inspired by Empress Alexandra Feodorovna's eighteenth-century English version attributed to James Cox (the former in the Hillwood Museum and Gardens, Washington, D.C., the latter in the Walters Art Gallery, Baltimore, MD), or the Louis XVI oval enameled box by Mikhail Perkhin, emulating the similar snuffbox in the Emperor's collection by eighteenth-century French goldsmith Joseph-Étienne Blerzy (both in the Forbes Magazine Collection, New York).
2. (1672-1725)
3. For a more general discussion of the Wigström workshop, *see* Ulla Tillander-Godenhielm's chapter in the present book; for a more general discussion of the styles of Fabergé in the album, *see* Alice Milica Ilich's article.
4. Grandjean, 1981, catalog no. 12.
5. Grandjean et al., 1975, catalog no. 117.
6. Ibid, catalog no. 122.
7. Ibid, p.285.
8. James Cracraft, 1997. See for example pp.226, 249, 252.
9. Schaffer, 1997.
10. Pauzié (1716-79), like many artists in Russia at this time, came from abroad: born in Switzerland, he moved to St. Petersburg at a young age. Wigström came from Finland, a country that was under Russian control at that time and quite close to St. Peters-

burg. Fabergé was of course born in Russia.
11. Berry-Hill et al., 1953, p.184.
12. Snowman, 1966, ill. 613-15.
13. Berry-Hill et al., op. cit., pp.180-1. The box is now in the Smithsonian Institution, Washington, D.C.
14. Snowman, 1966, op. cit., ill. 620.
15. Kaganov, 1997, p.1.
16. von Habsburg-Lothringen, 1983. p.36.
17. Cracraft, 1997, op. cit., p.249.
18. von Solodkoff, 1981, p.140.
19. Kaganov, 1997, op. cit., p.11.
20. Cracraft, 1997, op. cit., plate 33.
21. *The Neva Symphony*, 1975.
22. Belkova, 1993, pp.33-41.
23. Kaganov, 1997, op. cit., p.127.
24. *Panorama of Nevsky Prospect*, 1974.
25. Villumsen Krog, 1994, catalog no. 28.
26. Schaffer, ed., 1991, catalog no. 71.
27. Kaganov, 1997, op. cit., p.3.
28. Russian Museum, St. Petersburg.
29. Petrov, 1975.
30. Silverman, 1989, pp.159-71. *see* also Alice Milica Ilich's article.
31. Kaganov, 1997, op. cit., p.141.
32. Special thanks to Professor Richard Wortman of Columbia University, New York, for helpful discussions on this subject.
33. Schaffer, 1997, op. cit.
34. Snowman, 1962, plate XXX.
35. Snowman, ed., 1977, catalog no. H10.
36. von Habsburg, 1996, catalog no. 19. The box contains the hallmark for 1908-1917.
37. Krairiksh, ed., probably 1986, p.167.
38. von Habsburg, 1986-7, catalog no. 59
39. Virginia Museum of Fine Arts, Richmond. Bequest of Lillian Thomas Pratt.
40. From the period of the album.
41. von Habsburg et al., 1993, catalog no. 256.
42. *See* chapter 3 by Peter L. Schaffer.
43. Krairiksh, ed., probably 1986, p.195.

44. von Habsburg et al., 1993, op. cit., catalog no. 83; Snowman, 1962, op. cit., ill. no. 91; Habsburg, 1996, op. cit., catalog no. 82; Snowman, 1962, op. cit., ill. nos. 123-7.
45. von Habsburg-Lothringen et al., 1979, p.105.
46. Similar to one at the Stock Exchange in St. Petersburg.
47. von Habsburg, 1996, op. cit., catalog no. 70.
48. Professor Richard Wortman, personal communication.

Bibliography

Books and articles

BELKOVA, Guelia. "Saint-Pétersbourg au Temps des Tsars", in *Fabergé*, a special edition of *Connaissance des Arts*, Paris, 1993.
BERRY-HILL, Henry et al. *Antique Gold Boxes: Their Lore and Their Lure*, Abelard Press, New York, 1953.
CRACRAFT, James. *The Petrine Revolution in Russian Imagery*, University of Chicago Press, 1997.
GRANDJEAN, S. et al. *The James A. de Rothschild Collection at Waddesdon Manor: Gold Boxes and Miniatures of the Eighteenth Century*, London, 1975.
GRANDJEAN, Serge. *Catalogue des tabatières, boîtes étuis des XVIIIᵉ et XIXᵉ siècles du musée du Louvre*, Paris, 1981.
VON HABSBURG-LOTHRINGEN, Géza et al. *Fabergé*. Rizzoli, 1979.
VON HABSBURG-LOTHRINGEN, Géza. *Gold Boxes from the Collection of Rosalinde and Arthur Gilbert*, 1983.
VON HABSBURG, Géza. *Fabergé*. Catalog of an exhibition at the Kunsthalle, Munich, 1986-7, Geneva, 1987.
VON HABSBURG, Géza et al. *Fabergé: Imperial Jeweller*. Catalog of an exhibition at the State Hermitage Museum, 1993.
VON HABSBURG, Géza. *Fabergé in America*, Thames and Hudson, New York, 1996.
KAGANOV, Grigory. *Images of Space: St. Petersburg in the Visual and Verbal Arts*, Stanford University Press, 1997.

KRAIRIKSH, Busaya, ed. *Fabergé*, Office of Her Majesty's Private Secretary, Bangkok.
Panorama of Nevsky Prospect, Aurora Art Publishers, Leningrad, 1974.
PETROV, Vsevolod. *Mir Iskusstva*, Izobrazitelnoie Iskusstva, Moscow, 1975.
SCHAFFER, Paul, ed. *An Imperial Fascination: Porcelain – Dining with the Czars, Peterhof*, Catalog of an exhibition of services from the Russian imperial palaces, A La Vieille Russie, New York, 1991.
SCHAFFER, Paul. "The Art of Giving: the Presentation Piece in the Russian Decorative Arts", pp.15-24, in the catalog of the *International Fine Art and Antique Dealers Show*, New York, 1997.
SILVERMAN, Deborah L. *Art Nouveau in Fin-de-Siècle France*, University of California Press, 1989.
SNOWMAN, A. Kenneth. *The Art of Carl Fabergé*, London, 1962.
SNOWMAN, A. Kenneth. *Eighteenth Century Gold Boxes of Europe*, London, 1966.
SNOWMAN, A. Kenneth, ed. *Fabergé, 1846-1920*. Catalog of an exhibition at the Victoria and Albert Museum, London, 1977.
VON SOLODKOFF, Alexander. *Russian Gold and Silverwork: 17ᵗʰ-19ᵗʰ Century*, Rizzoli, 1981.
The Neva Symphony: Leningrad in Works of Graphic Art and Painting, Aurora Art Publishers, Leningrad, 1975.
VILLUMSEN KROG, Ole, ed. *Imperial Easter Eggs: An Exhibition of Porcelain Easter Eggs*, Catalog of an exhibition at Christiansborg Palace, Copenhagen, 1994.

Personal communications
HILTON, Alison, Associate Professor of Art History, Georgetown University.
KASINEC, Edward, Chief Curator of the Slavic and Baltic Division of the New York Public Library, New York.
WORTMAN, Richard, Professor of History, Columbia University, New York.

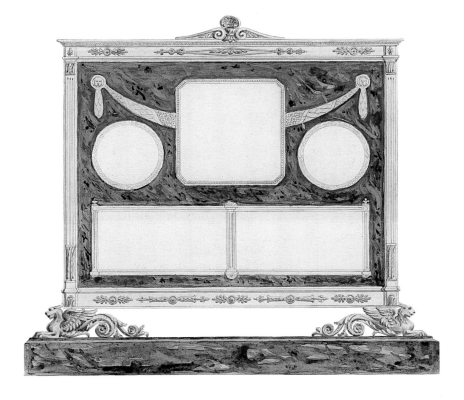

Drawing of an Empire-style
multiple frame in nephrite,
gold, gilded silver and enamel.

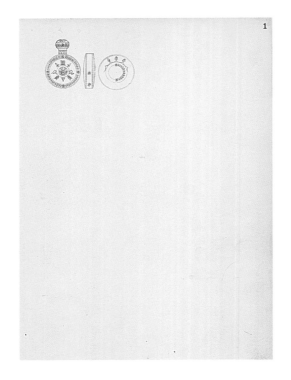

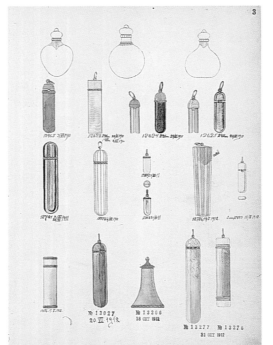

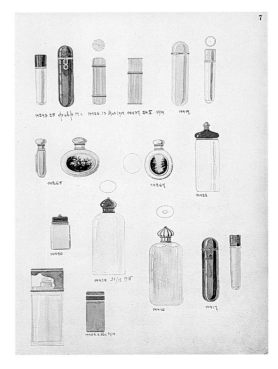

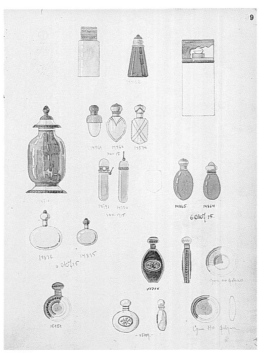

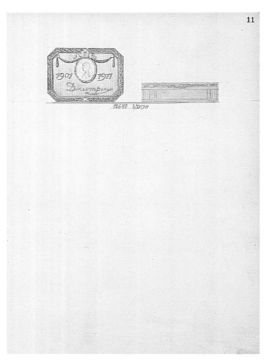

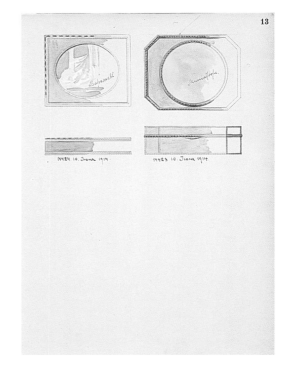

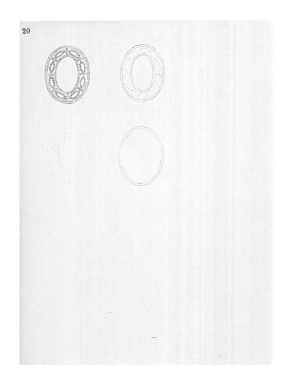

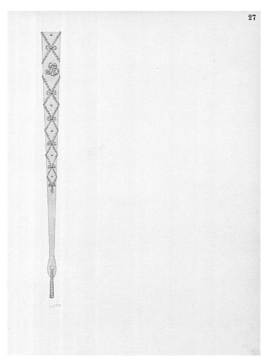

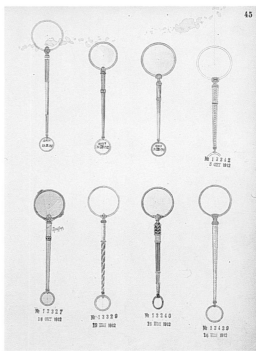

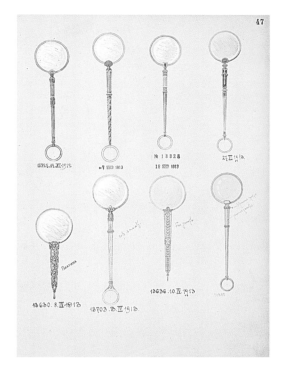

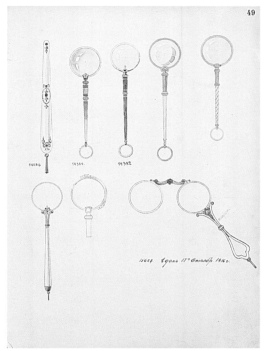

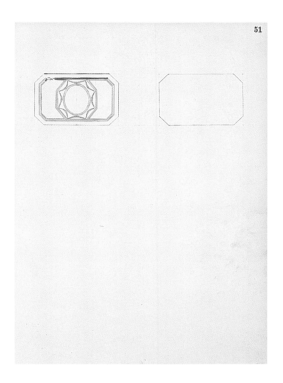

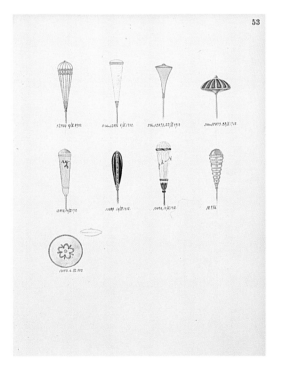

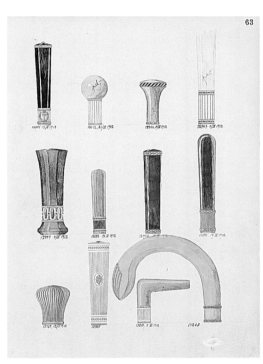

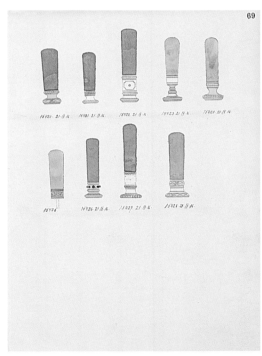

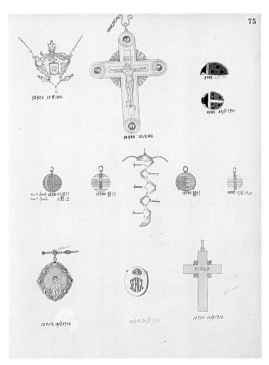

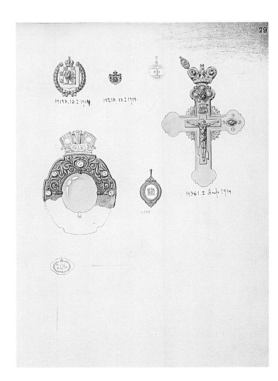

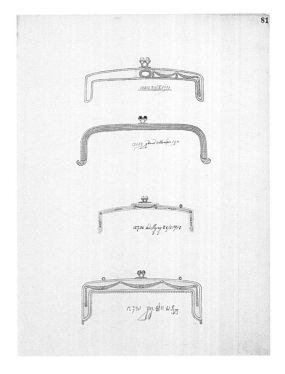

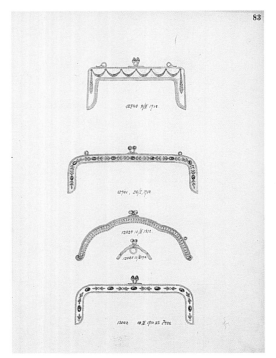

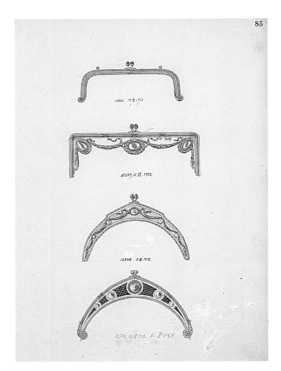

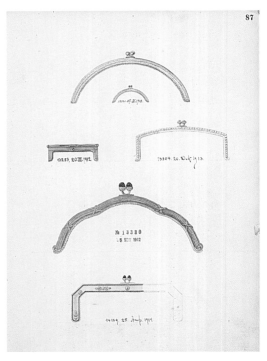

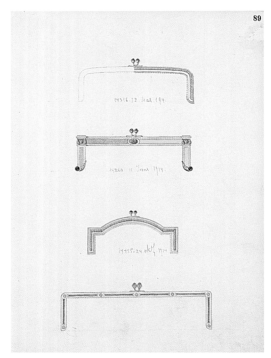

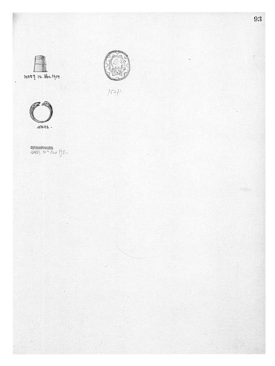

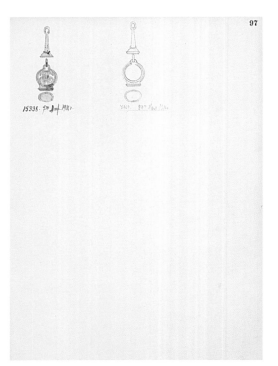

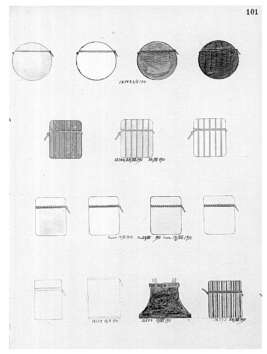

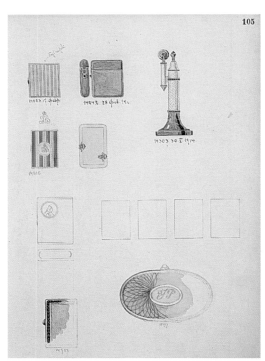

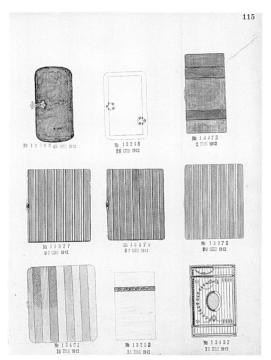

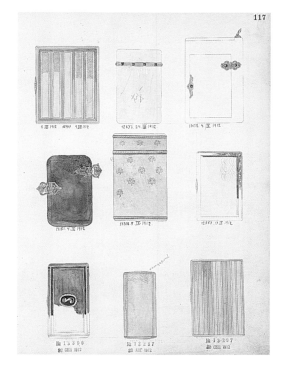

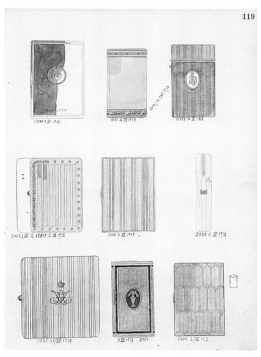

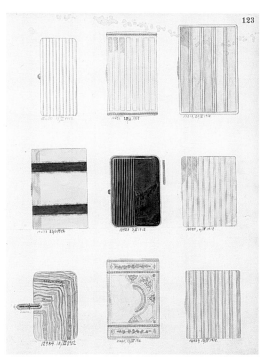

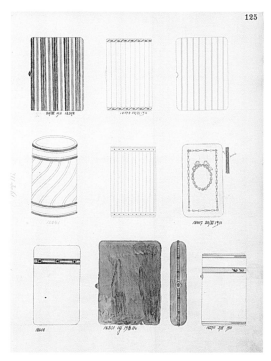

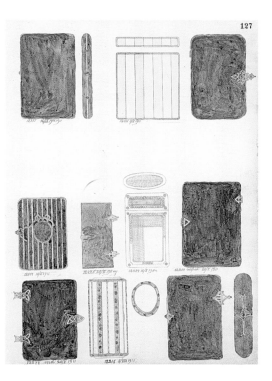

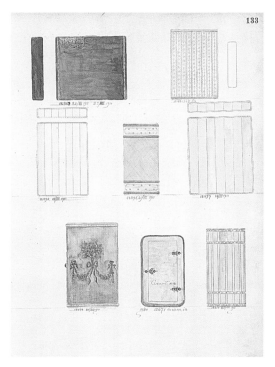

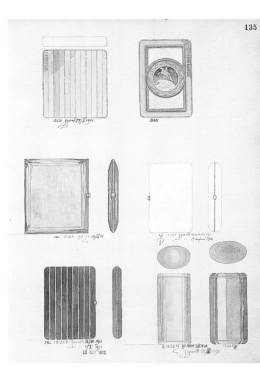

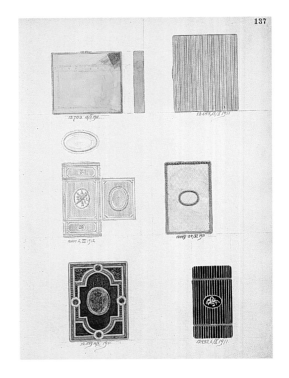

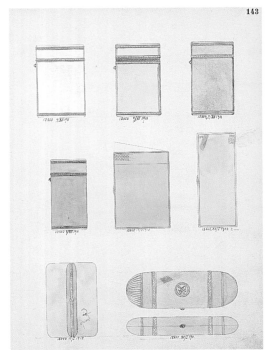

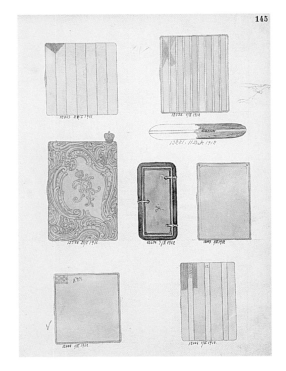

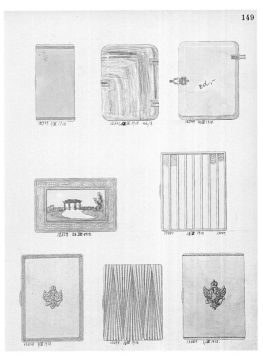

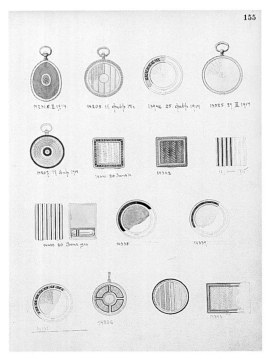

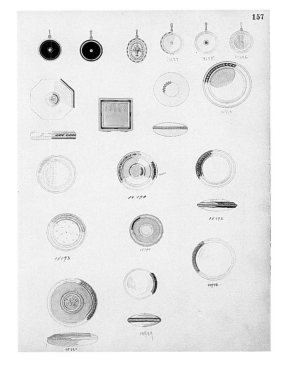

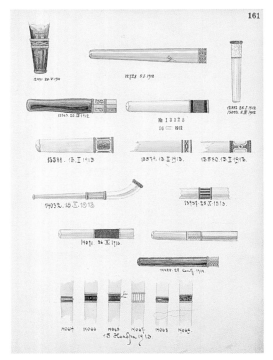

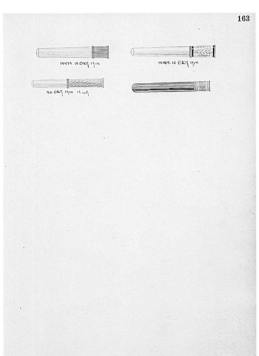

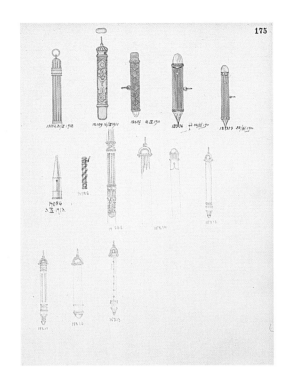

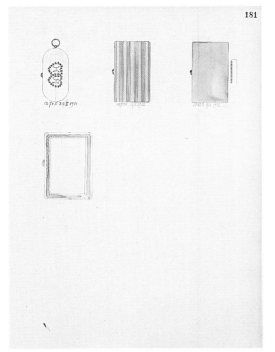

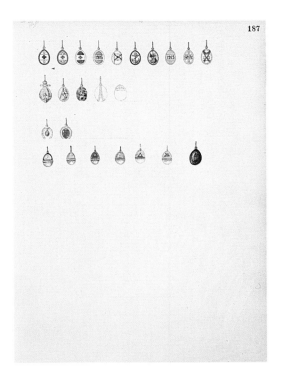

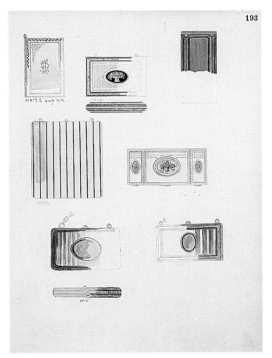

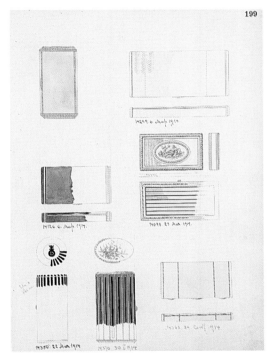

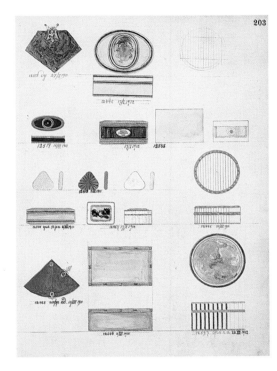

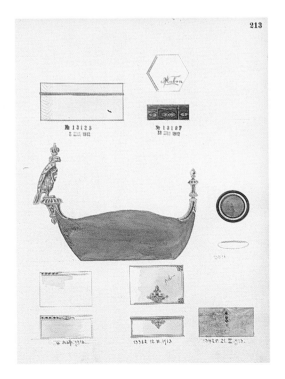

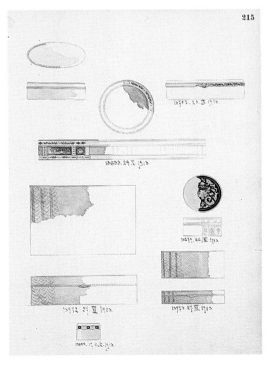

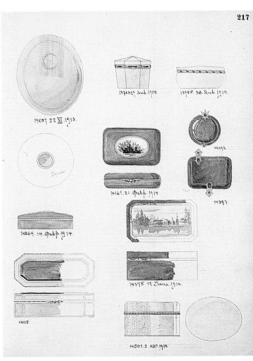

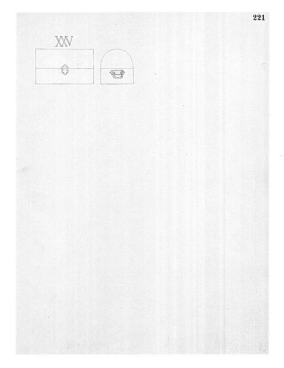

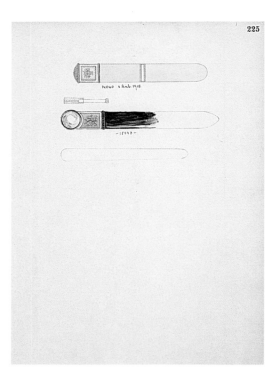

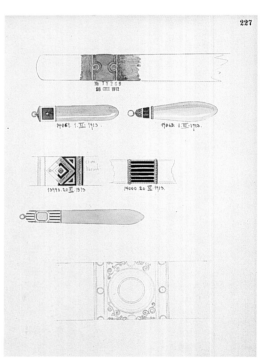

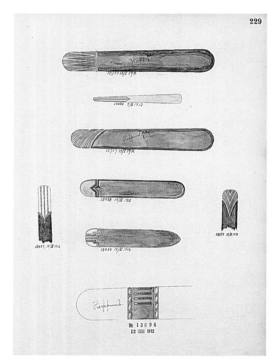

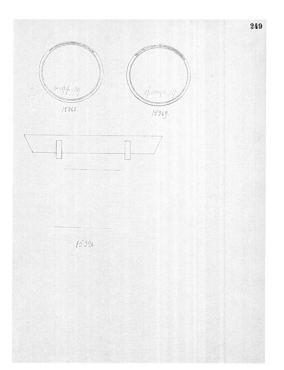

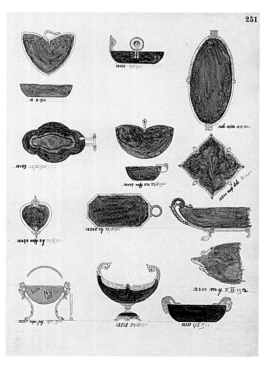

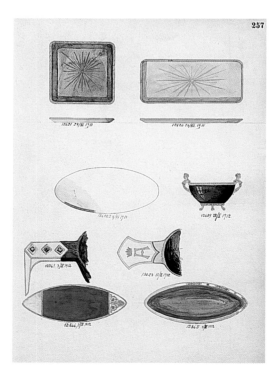

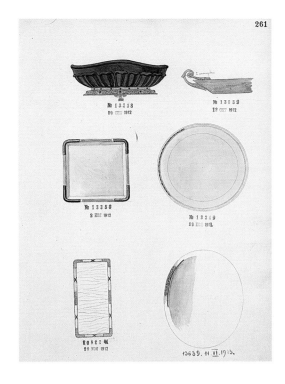

261

275

285

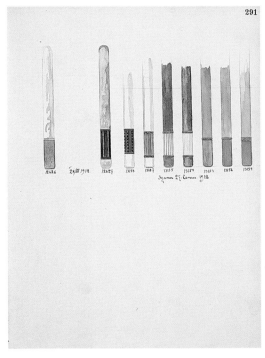

291

297

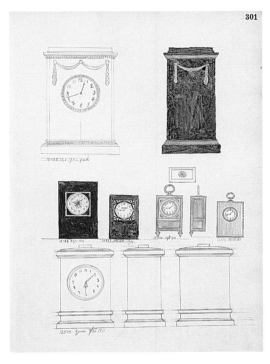

301

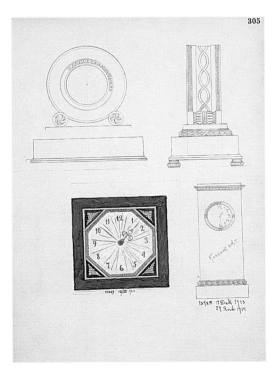

305

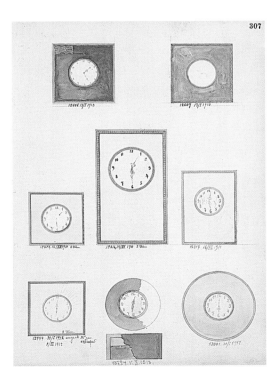

307

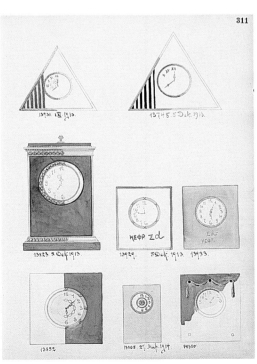

311

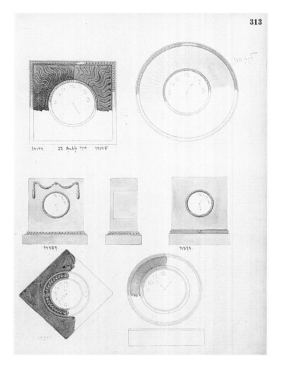

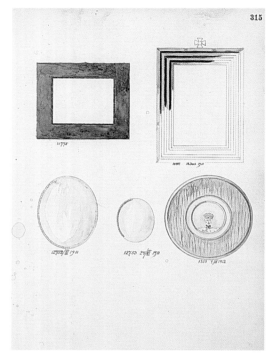

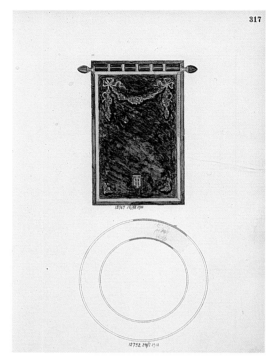

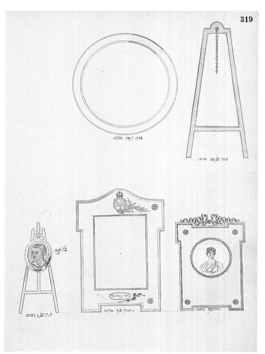

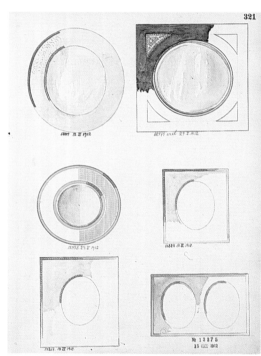

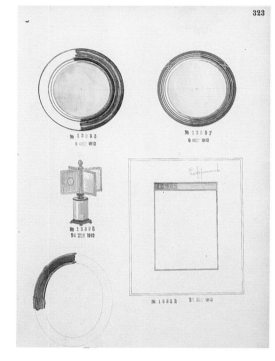

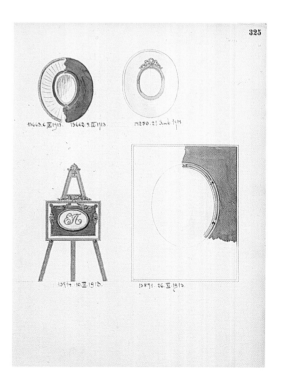

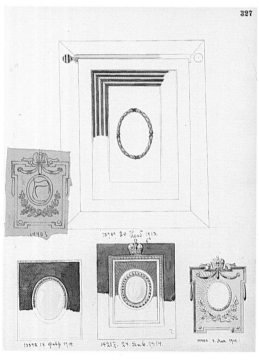

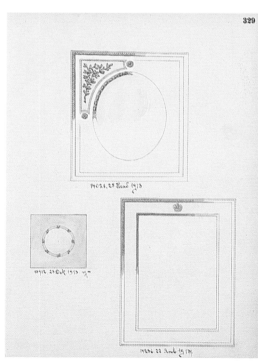

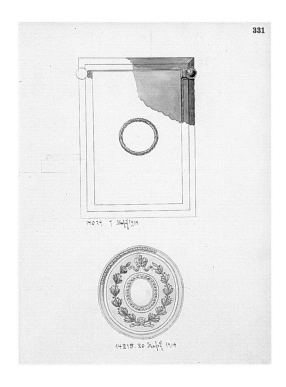

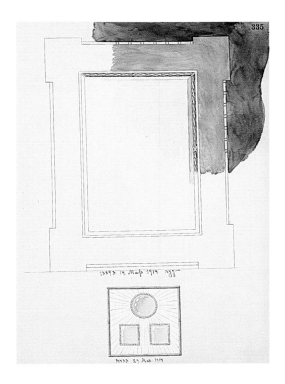

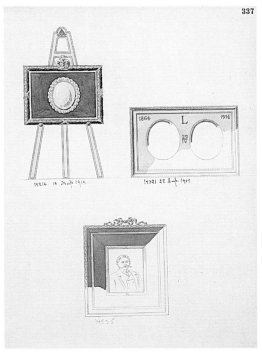

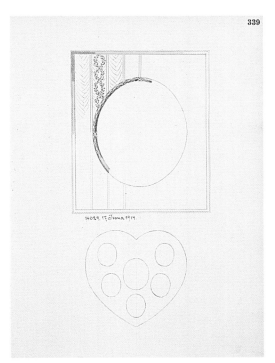

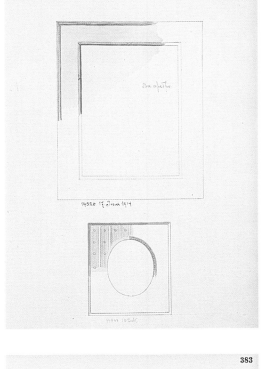

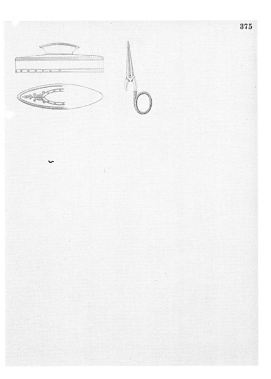

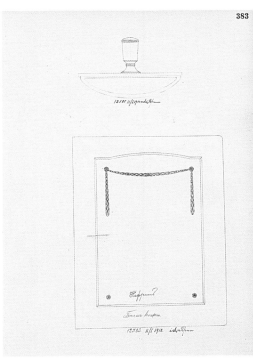

The original plates of the Wigström album measure 16-3/8 x 11-5/8 inches (41.6 x 29.5 centimeters) and the drawings featured on them show the objects at their are actual size. Plates reproduced here at full-page size are reproduced at 85% actual size, as are photographs of the pieces themselves (multiply by 1.18 to calculate actual size).

Particular drawings can be identified by the production number usually given below. Production numbers or details in square brackets indicate objects known to exist but not reproduced here. All plates and drawings photographed by Jean Chénel.

PLATE 1: see page 156
Pencil-drawn scent bottle

PLATE 3: see page 156
Scent bottles in hardstone and enamel; bowenite gum pot [13277]

PLATE 5: see page 15
Scents bottles and gum pots in hardstone, enamel, or crystal [13641]

PLATE 7: see page 156
Scent bottles in enamel, hardstone or varicolored gold
Drawings 14268 and 14267: see page 17

PLATE 9: see page 156
Scent bottles, some in nephrite, others in *guilloché* enamel

PLATE 11: see page 57
Gold box of Prince Dmitri Alexandrovich

PLATE 13: see page 80 (drawing 14424) and page 42 (drawing 14423)

PLATE 20: see page 156
Pencil-drawn miniature frames

PLATE 25: see page 18
Fan mounts

PLATE 27: see page 156
Fan mount in the neo-classical style with the owner's initials LB

PLATE 41: see page 19
Jeweled and enameled lorgnettes

PLATE 43: see page 22
Jeweled and enameled lorgnettes

PLATE 45: see page 156
Lorgnettes in the neo-classical style
Drawing 13327: see page 24
Drawing 13240: see page 25

PLATE 47: see page 157
Jeweled and enameled lorgnettes

PLATE 49: see page 157
Jeweled and enameled lorgnettes [Top row, fourth from left]

PLATE 51: see page 157
Pencil-drawn presentation box

PLATE 53: see page 157
Hat pins
Drawing 12899: in the Rothschild colors (blue and yellow); see page 126

PLATE 61: see page 28
Hardstone and eameled cane handles, most of them with details in the neo-classical style.

PLATE 63: see page 157
Cane handles and parasol handles
Drawing 13004: see page 30
Drawings 13210, 12906, 13042, 13169: see page 31

PLATE 65: see page 32
Cane handles and hand seals

PLATE 67: see page 35
Parasol and cane handles and hand seals
Drawing appearing on second line, second from right: presumably designed by E. Illinskaya-Andreolotti, second wife of Franz Birbaum, head designer at Fabergé

PLATE 69: see page 157
Hand seals with hardstone handles
Drawing 15422: see page 105

PLATE 73: see page 157
Pencil-drawn pendants with a frost-flower motif. Designed for the oil tycoon Emanuel Nobel by Alma Pihl, artist of the Albert Holmström workshop.

PLATE 75: see page 157
Jewelry [12782]
Drawing 12780: see page 59.
Drawing 12910: see page 59

PLATE 77: see page 38
Jewelry
Drawing 12983: with the enameled coat-of-arms of the Galitzin family

PLATE 79: see page 157
Commemmorative badges, pectoral cross and panagia
Drawing 14193: see page 46
Print bottom line: see page 66

PLATE 81: see page 158
Evening bag frames
[12736: the actual object is in the Royal Collection, Thailand]

PLATES 83, 85 AND 87: see page 158
Evening bag frames

PLATE 89: see page 158
Evening bag frames
[Bottom line: see page 126]

PLATE 91: see page 40
Jewelry

PLATE 93: see page 158
Thimble, pencil-drawn cameo brooch, ring.
Drawing 15249: see page 114

PLATE 97: see page 158
Seals

PLATE 101: see page 158
Match cases, match holder
Drawing 12563: see page 44
Drawing 12504: see page 45

PLATE 103: see page 49
Match cases, match boxes, match holder.

PLATE 105: see page 158
Match cases, table lighter
Drawing 14303: see page 67

PLATE 107: see page 62
Match case

PLATE 111: see page 159
Miniature animal figurines carved in hardstone [12530]

Drawing 12639: see page 51
Drawings 12637, 12523, and 12638: see page 78

PLATE 113: see page 50
Figurine: dark green and brown jasper, obsidian, grey and pink chalcedony, lapis-lazuli, sapphires, gold, silver, enamel and jet

PLATE 115: see page 159
Cigarette cases, some with a ribbed décor heralding modernism, the prevailing style of the 1920s

PLATE 117: see page 159
Cigarette cases

PLATE 119: see page 159
Cigarette cases
Drawing 13187: see page 55
Drawing 12701: see page 52

PLATE 121: see page 53
Cigarette cases in rock crystal, varicolored gold and enamel

PLATES 123 AND 125 [12732]: see page 159
Cigarette cases

PLATE 127: see page 159
Cigarette cases, some designed in a style heralding Art Deco
Drawing bottom line, second from left: see page 52

PLATE 129: see page 54
Cigarette cases in nephrite, enamel and gold [12427]

PLATE 131: see page 56
Cigarette cases in rock crystal, nephrite, enamel and gold

PLATE 133: see page 159
Cigarette cases

PLATE 135: see page 159
Cigarette cases
Drawing 12401: a similar case in the collection of H.M. Queen Elizabeth II, originally purchased by Queen Mary from Prince Vladimir Galitzin and presented to King George V for Christmas, 1934
Drawing 12362: see page 167 (opposite)

PLATE 137: see page 160
Cigarette cases
Drawing 12600: see page 101

PLATE 139: see page 60
Cigarette cases in varicolored gold, hardstone or enamel

PLATE 141: see page 64
Cigarette cases in enamel, nephrite and varicolored gold

PLATE 143: see page 160
Cigarette cases and a gold case
[12855: see p.168]

PLATE 145: see page 160
Cigarette cases
Drawing 12798: see page 62

PLATE 147: see page 69
Cigarette cases

PLATE 149: see page 160
Cigarette cases
Drawing 12872: see page 101
Drawing 13030: see page 44

PLATE 151: see page 70
Fob watches, lockets, compacts

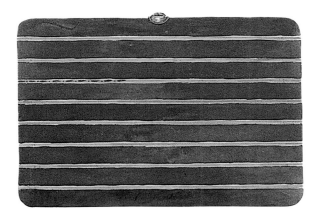

Drawing of a gold cigarette case with blue enamel stripes, taken from plate 135.

Drawings of a case in polished and *guilloché* gold, taken from plate 143.

All objects are by Fabergé, workmaster Henrik
Wigström, hallmarked for St. Petersburg 1908-17,
unless otherwise indicated.
Objects featured in the album are reproduced at 85%
actual size (multiply by 1.18 to calculate actual size).

CHAPTER I. HENRIK WIGSTRÖM

Page 12

The Wigström album and separate working drawings found therewith.
Photograph: Studio Sempre - Harri Kosonen

Page 14

Enamel gum pot
Courtesy of Dr. Edwin I. Radlauer, New York
Photograph: Helga Photo Studio

Bowenite gum pot
Wartski, London
Photograph: Wartski, London

Page 16

Drawing of a nephrite frame in the neo-classical
style.
Private collection
Photograph: Jean Chénel

Page 17

Scent flask
Private collection
Photograph: Courtesy of Michel Ghosn

Page 20

Nevsky Prospekt
Royal Archives, Windsor Castle
© Royal Archives - Her Majesty Queen Elizabeth II

Page 21

Carl Fabergé sorting gemstones
Photograph: Courtesy of Wartski, London

Henrik Wigström's workshop
Photograph: Courtesy of Wartski, London

The Fabergé building on Bolshaya Morskaya Ulitsa
Photograph: Courtesy of Wartski, London

Page 23

Gold lorgnette
Courtesy of Dr. Edwin I. Radlauer, New York
Photograph: Helga Photo Studio

Grand Duchess Elizaveta Feodorovna's lorgnette
The FORBES Magazine Collection, New York
All rights reserved
Photograph: Larry Stein

Grand Duchess Elizaveta Feodorovna
Royal Archives, Windsor Castle
© Royal Archives - Her Majesty Queen Elizabeth II

Page 24

Platinum lorgnette
Private collection
Photograph: Helga Photo Studio

Page 25

Fragments and semi-manufactured objects
Private collection
Photograph: Helga Photo Studio

Page 26

Henrik Wigström
Courtesy of Anni Sarvi

Page 27

The Wigström children
Courtesy of Anni Sarvi

Ida Wigström
Courtesy of Anni Sarvi

Page 29

Enamel compact
Private collection
Photograph: Courtesy of Wartski, London

Parasol handle
Private collection
Photograph: Helga Photo Studio

Page 33

Triple nephrite seal
Private collection
Photograph: Helga Photo Studio

Enamel hand seal
Private collection
Photograph: Wartski, London

The Fabergé sales room
Courtesy of Wartski, London

Page 34

Topaz handle
The State Hermitage Museum, St. Petersburg
Photograph: Svetlana Soujetova
© 2000 The State Hermitage Museum, St. Petersburg

Smoky quartz handle
Provenance: study of Nicholas II in the
Alexander Palace at Tsarsköe Selo
Kremlin Armory, Moscow Kremlin State
Museum-Preserve of History and Culture
Photograph: Rauno Träskelin, Museum of Art and
Design, Helsinki

Page 36

Working drawing (top left)
Courtesy of Pekka Haikonen

Cigarette case
Private collection
Photograph: Rauno Träskelin, Museum of Art and
Design, Helsinki

Working drawing (bottom right)
Courtesy of Pekka Haikonen

Page 37

Box with turquoise cover
Private collection
Photograph: Helga Photo Studio

Locket
A La Vieille Russie
Photograph: Helga Photo Studio

Page 39

Hardstone figurine (pirozhnik)
Private collection
Photograph: Helga Photo Studio

The Wigström family dacha
Courtesy Anni Sarvi

CHAPTER II. PATRONS OF PRESTIGE

Page 41

Caricature of Count Mikhail Nikolaievich Grabbe
The Russian National Library, St. Petersburg
Photograph: The Russian National Library,
St. Petersburg

The Beloselsky-Belozersky Palace
Royal Archives, Windsor Castle
© Royal Archives - Her Majesty Queen Elizabeth II

Page 43

Empress Alexandra Feodorovna
Courtesy of Marvin Lyons

Imperial presentation box
Private collection
Photograph: Rauno Träskelin, Museum of Art and
Design, Helsinki

Page 44

Enamel match case.
Private collection
Photograph: Courtesy of Michel Ghosn

Page 45

Bowenite match holder
Private collection
Photograph: Helga Photo Studio

Page 48

Match case in the Rothschild colors
Private collection
Photograph: Helga Photo Studio

Enamel match case
Private collection
Photograph: Helga Photo Studio

Page 51

A.A. Kudinov helping Dowager Empress Maria
Feodorovna
The State Pavlovsk Palace Museum, St. Petersburg
Photograph: © The State Pavlovsk Palace Museum,
St. Petersburg

Kudinov figurine
The State Pavlovsk Palace Museum, St. Petersburg
Photograph: © The State Pavlovsk Palace Museum,
St. Petersburg

Agate owl
The Woolf Family Collection
Photograph: Prudence Cummings, London

Page 52

Cigarette holder (mundstuck)
Courtesy of Dr. Edwin I. Radlauer, New York
Photograph: Helga Photo Studio

Page 55

Grand Duchess Victoria Feodorovna and Grand
Duke Kirill Vladimirovich
Courtesy of Marvin Lyons

Pink enamel cigarette case
Collection John Traina
Photograph: Fred Lyon

Page 57

Prince Dmitri Alexandrovich
Courtesy of Marvin Lyons

CHAPTER III. FABERGÉ AND
THE ROYAL COLLECTION OF THAILAND

Nephrite Buddha
Private collection
Photograph: Helga Photo Studio

Page 92

King Mongkut's miniature
Workmaster: Albert Holmström (attributed)
The Royal Collection, Thailand.
Courtesy of H.M.'s private secretary

Nephrite box
The Royal Collection, Thailand.
Photograph: Helga Photo Studio

Page 94

Gold and enamel cigarette case
The Royal Collection, Thailand
Photograph: Helga Photo Studio

Cigarette holder (from the cigarette case shown on
the same page)
The Royal Collection, Thailand,
Photograph: Helga Photo Studio

Page 95

The Temple of Dawn — *Wat Arun* — in Bangkok
Photograph: Helga Photo Studio

Temple of Dawn box
The Royal Collection, Thailand.
Photograph: Helga Photo Studio

Page 96

Nephrite Buddha
Private collection
Photograph: Helga Photo Studio

Miniature sledge
The Royal Collection, Thailand.
Photograph: Helga Photo Studio

Page 97

Nephrite cup
The Royal Collection, Thailand
Photograph: Helga Photo Studio

CHAPTER IV. THE TRIUMPH OF STYLE

Page 99

Rhodonite box
The FORBES Magazine Collection, New York.
All rights reserved
Photograph: Larry Stein

Miniature bidet (salt chair)
© The Cleveland Museum of Art, 1999, the India
Early Minshall Collection, 1966.455
Photograph: The Cleveland Museum of Art

Page 100

Imperial presentation box in nephrite
Private collection
Photograph: Prudence Cummings, London

Snuffbox, Wartski, London
Photograph: Prudence Cummings, London

Countess de Hohenfelzen, later Princess Paley
Collection of Prince Michel Romanoff

Page 101

Matilda Kshesinskaia
St. Petersburg State Museum of Theatre and Music

Nephrite cigarette case
Private collection
Photograph: Prudence Cummings, London

Miniature armchair
The FORBES Magazine Collection, New York.
All rights reserved
Photograph: Joseph Coscia, Jr.

Stamp box, A La Vieille Russie
Photograph: Helga Photo Studio

Pentagonal nephrite box
Collection Joan and Melissa Rivers
Photograph: Courtesy of Joan and Melissa Rivers

Page 104

Lion Bridge in St. Petersburg
Photograph: Alexander Berman

Rhodonite table clock
Private collection
Photograph: Helga Photo Studio

Page 105

Lapis lazuli hand seal
Private collection
Photograph: Helga Photo Studio

The Isidore Yurievsky church in St. Petersburg
Photograph: Alexander Berman

Page 108

Nephrite box
Private collection
Photograph: Helga Photo Studio

Red enamel table box
A La Vieille Russie
Photograph: Helga Photo Studio

Page 109

Madame Dmitri Vonliarliarsky
From *Album du bal costumé au Palais d'Hiver, février 1903*
The Russian National Library, St. Petersburg

Miniature gold samovar
The Woolf Family Collection
Photograph: Prudence Cummings, London

Page 110

Chinese nephrite cricket cage
The Woolf Family Collection
Photograph: Prudence Cummings, London

Wat Arun - Temple of Dawn table box
The Royal Collection, Thailand.
Photograph: Helga Photo Studio

Page 114

Nephrite paperknife
The Woolf Family Collection
Photograph: Prudence Cummings, London

Nephrite bowl,
A La Vieille Russie
Photograph: Helga Photo Studio

Page 115

Lapis lazuli bowl
The Woolf Family Collection
Photograph: Prudence Cummings, London

Page 118

Harlequin snuffbox

A La Vieille Russie
Photograph: Helga Photo Studio

Page 120

Emperor Nicholas II and members of the Imperial
family. From left to right: Prince Piotr Oldenburg,
Empress Alexandra Feodorovna, Grand Duke
Vladimir Alexandrovich, Grand Duchess Olga
Alexandrovna, Emperor Nicholas II, Grand Duke
Mikhail Alexandrovich, Grand Duke Boris
Vladimirovich, Prince Gavriil Konstantinovich,
Prince Ioann Konstantinovich, Grand Duke
Andrei Vladimirovich and Duke George von
Meckenburg-Strelitz.
The Russian National Library, St. Petersburg

Miniature nephrite water bucket
Private Collection
Photograph: Helga Photo Studio

Page 121 - Plate 263

Nephrite presentation kovsh
A La Vieille Russie
Photograph : Helga Photo Studio

Page 122

Rhodonite box
Private collection
Photograph: Prudence Cummings, London

Nephrite cup
Virginia Museum of Fine Arts, Richmond. Bequest
of Lillian Thomas Pratt. Acc. No. 47 20 295
Photograph: Katherine Wetzel
© Virginia Museum of Fine Arts

Page 124

Hoarfrost
Photograph: Reino Turunen

Page 126

Lapis lazuli table clock
A La Vieille Russie
Photograph: Helga Photo Studio

Page 129

Bowenite ashtray
The FORBES Magazine Collection, New York
All rights reserved
Photograph: H. Peter Curran

Miniature carriage clock with opaque white enamel
stripes
Private collection
Photograph: Wartski, London

Enamel bellpush
Courtesy of Dr. Edwin I. Radlauer, New York
Photograph: Helga Photo Studio

CHAPTER V. IMAGES OF ST. PETERSBURG

Page 133

Purpurine table clock
A La Vieille Russie
Photograph : Helga Photo Studio

Nephrite table clock
© The Cleveland Museum of Art, 1999, the India
Early Minshall Collection, 1966.475
Photograph: The Cleveland Museum of Art

Rhodonite box mounted
à cage in gold, with
the border of green enamel
enclosing white enamel
dots, similar to an example
shown on plate 203.

The FORBES Magazine
Collection, New York,
holds this Imperial
presentation tray with
marks of both workmasters
Henrik Wigström and
his mentor Mikhail Perkhin.

The publisher and authors would like to express their thanks to the many generous people who have helped in the production of this volume. They are particularly grateful for the gracious support of Her Majesty Queen Sirikit of Thailand.

Anni Sarvi, granddaughter of Henrik Wigström, has generously made available her family archives and albums and shared her memories and knowledge of life in imperial St.Petersburg. Without the enthusiasm and patience of Amy Spiik and her mother Mirjam Kagan, former neighbor of the Wigström family, this project would never have come so far.

At the New Orleans Museum of Art, we are indebted to E. John Bullard III, Director, John W. Keefe, Curator of Decorative Arts, and to Paul Tarver, Registrar, whose cooperation and support have been both generous and indispensable.

At the State Pavlovsk Palace Museum, our special thanks are due to the Director, Nikolai S. Tretiakov, and to the Head Curator, Alexei N. Guzanov who has provided helpful suggestions and photographs. At the Moscow Kremlin State Museum of History and Culture, we are grateful to the General Director Irina A. Rodimtseva, to Tatiana N. Muntian, Curator of the Nineteenth-Century Russian Jewelry at the Armory Museum, and to Irina F. Polynina, Head of the "Diamond Fund Exhibition". At the State Hermitage Museum, we owe special thanks to the Director, Professor Mikhail B. Piotrovsky and his Deputies Dr. Georgi V. Vilinbakhov and Dr. Vladimir Y. Matveiev, to Dr. Marina N. Lopato, Curator of Western Applied Art, to Larissa A. Zavadskaia, Curator of Western Art and to Karina A. Orlova. At the Musée des Arts Décoratifs, Paris, we are grateful for the kind assistance of Mme Evelyne Possémé, Curator, Mme Sonia Edard, Mlle Rachel Brishoual and Mlle Carol Chabert.

At the St. Petersburg State Museum of Theatre and Music, we are indebted for their valuable assistance to the Deputy Director, Natalia Metelitsa, Dr. Marina Godlevskaya, Head of Opera and Photography, Julia Rybakova, Curator of Photography, Elina Samkova, Head of Rare Books, and Anna Shoulgat, Assistant to the Director. We also thank Dr. Elena V. Barkhatova of the Russian National Library, St. Petersburg. Our appreciation goes to Anita J. Ellis, Acting Director of the Cincinnati Art Museum, and to Jennifer Howe, Assistant Curator of Decorative Arts; to Frances Dimond, Curator of the Photographic Collection of the Royal Archives, Windsor Castle; to the Witt Library, Courtauld Institute of Art, London; to the National Portrait Gallery, London, and to the Rothschild Archive, London. A. Kenneth Snowman of Wartski, one of our early supporters, and his close collaborators Geoffrey Munn, Katherine Purcell and Kieran McCarthy, have contributed valuable information and material. At the FORBES Magazine Collection, we owe special thanks to Christopher Forbes, Margaret Trombly and Robin Tromeur-Brenner; and we are indebted also to the Woolf Family Collection, to Dr. Edwin I. Radlauer, to Joan and Melissa Rivers, to John Traina, to Chevalier Meurice F. Mizzi, to Mme Xenia Cheremeteff-Sfiri, and to many generous private collectors.

Finally, we owe a deep debt of gratitude to the following individuals, all of whom have made invaluable contributions in innumerable ways:
Valentin V. Skurlov, who has been a most important collaborator, tirelessly offering archival research in St. Petersburg; Marvin Lyons, with his vast knowledge of the history of Imperial Russia, its social and military institutions, an untiring supporter, the source of much information and rare photographic material for the chapter on Fabergé's clientele; Barbro Schauman, an active participant in the research of the first two chapters, who has provided inspiring comments throughout the preparation of this work; Tatiana Fabergé, great granddaughter of Fabergé, for primary details from her family archives; Dr. Edward Kasinec, Chief Curator of the Slavic and Baltic Division of the New York Library, for continuous help and generosity; Ambassador F.L. Kellogg, Chairman of the U.S. Committee of the *Thai Support Foundation*, an enthusiastic supporter; Larissa Lockwood, an inspired help to the writing and research; Jacques Ferrand, for sharing his deep knowledge of Imperial Russian history.
We also wish to thank: members of the staff of A La Vieille Russie, as well as Jean-Jacques Journet, Xavier Chiron, Prince Emmanuel de Broglie, Jean Chénel, Thomas Cobbe, Gavin Harding, M. and Mme Michel Escourbiac, Alain Escourbiac, Philippe Escourbiac, Claude Mastantuono and Catherine Challot.
Many of those named above and many private collectors who wish to remain anonymous, have generously offered pieces on loan to the exhibition coinciding with the publication of this book, at A La Vieille Russie and the New Orleans Museum of Art.

ALAIN DE GOURCUFF ÉDITEUR
ULLA TILLANDER-GODENHIELM
ALICE MILICA ILICH
PETER L. SCHAFFER, MARK A. SCHAFFER

AUTHORS' ACKNOWLEDGMENTS

Working on this book has been a labor of love, not only for myself, but also for many close friends and colleagues in practically all corners of the world. In addition to those named above, my gratitude also goes to Oleg A. Fabergé's family in Helsinki for their friendly support. Alexis de Tiesenhausen has found information on innumerable objects depicted in the album, and has given much kind assistance. My thanks for valuable help go also to Timothy F. Boettger, Christel McCanless, Stephen Dale, Pekka Haikonen, Magnus Liljequist, Will Lowes, Olga Ousova, Arvi Palohcimo, Marilyn Pfeifer Swezey, Andre Ruzhnikov, Lucy Söderström, Pehr Wallin and Michael Wynne-Ellis. My husband Lars-Petter Godenhielm deserves a very special mention for his stoic tolerance and his unfailing encouragement. And last but by no means least comes my father, the jeweler Herbert Tillander, today one of the last survivors of the goldsmiths' art of imperial St. Petersburg. Up until his ninth birthday in 1918 the world described in this book was his.

ULLA TILLANDER-GODENHIELM

My contribution to this book is dedicated to my parents, Sofia and Milorad Ilich.
I owe my involvement in this remarkable project entirely to my close friend and former colleague, Barbro Schauman. The close working relationship formed from the outset between Ulla Tillander-Godenhielm, Barbro Schauman and myself has been punctuated by many memorable moments in St. Petersburg and London, as well as in their beautiful homes in Finland. I wish to thank their respective families, and in particular their husbands, Lars-Petter and Jan-Henrik, for their great humor, patience and support. To Barbro, I wish to offer special thanks for her untiring enthusiasm and continuous flow of interesting ideas and suggestions. To Ulla, I wish to express my appreciation for the opportunity to work with such a delightful, inspiring and professional colleague.
John J. Medveckis, Herbert Ypma, Nicholas Brawer, Maggi Smith, Martin Schwartz and Larrimore Hampton, Hans and Jagoda Wuttke and all the members of Wartski's have each offered valuable encouragement, advice and support. I wish to thank Prince Michel Romanoff for generously bringing to our attention previously unknown family photographs. Larissa Lockwood and the many Fabergé collectors who have kindly lent their support have also made valuable contributions to this book.

ALICE MILICA ILICH

Above all, I wish to thank Her Majesty Queen Sirikit for her gracious support in the production of this volume and the accompanying exhibition. Her *Thai Support Foundation*, which benefits from this book, carries out a great deal of work on behalf of the Thai people and their native culture. My thanks also to Thanpying Parani Mahanonda for her assistance during my visit to Thailand to photograph the collection and select pieces featured in the Wigström album. Her Majesty Queen Sirikit's volume (*c*.1986) on the entire Royal Collection of Fabergé and the relationship between His Majesty and the Emperor, which she describes as a "gesture of honor to His Late Majesty King Chulalongkorn", was of great assistance in my research.
I owe a special debt to Khunying Yoopa Pranich, a dear friend and "sister" of many years who has been tireless in her efforts and enthusiasm for this book and the accompanying exhibition. I have learned a great deal from her and from her husband Kanok.

PETER L. SCHAFFER

Paul Schaffer, my father, and Peter L. Schaffer, my uncle, were both convinced from the outset of the significance of Ulla Tillander-Godenhielm's discovery and her extraordinary work, and of the importance of bringing Wigström's album to the attention of the public, accompanied by detailed discussions and analysis. Their mentoring of my education in Fabergé's work has been even more important, as they have shared with me their passion for beautiful objects, informed by the breadth and depth of their knowledge and experience. The chapter I have contributed to this book has benefited particularly from my father's intelligent and careful comments and discussions. In addition to those already thanked above, I should like to express my gratitude to Director Vadim V. Znamenov and Chief Curator Nina V. Vernova, respectively Director and Chief Curator of Peterhof and dear friends and supporters both; to Professor Richard Wortman of Columbia University, New York, who offered valuable insights into the importance of monuments in Russia at the beginning of the twentieth century; and so to Alison Hilton, Associate Professor of Art History at Georgetown University, Washington D.C., who provided useful suggestions.

MARK A. SCHAFFER

© 2000 A LA VIEILLE RUSSIE

Printed in 2000
for ALAIN de GOURCUFF ÉDITEUR

Editor: Barbara Mellor
Editorial assistant: Xavier Lacaille
Design: Maxence Scherf

Phototypeset, photogravure, and printing:
Imprimerie Escourbiac, Graulhet (Tarn), France

ISBN 2-909-838-47-1